CONFIGURATION BLUEPRINTS DYNAMICS AX 2012

Volume 1

BY

MURRAY FIFE

Preface

Errata

Although we have taken every care to ensure the accuracy of our content, mistakes do happen. If you find a mistake in one of our books—maybe a mistake in the text or the code—we would be grateful if you would report this to us. By doing so, you can save other readers from frustration and help us improve subsequent versions of this book. If you find any errata, please report them by emailing murray@murrayfife.me.

PIRACY

Piracy of copyright material on the Internet is an ongoing problem across all media. If you come across any illegal copies of our works, in any form, on the Internet, please provide us with the location address or website name immediately so that we can pursue a remedy.

Please contact us at murray@murrayfife.me with a link to the suspected pirated material.

We appreciate your help in protecting our authors, and our ability to bring you valuable content.

QUESTIONS

You can contact us at murray@murrayfife.me if you are having a problem with any aspect of the book, and we will do our best to address it.

Table of Contents

Introduction

Once you have mastered the core functions within Dynamics AX like Order To Cash, Procure To Pay, or Production you don't need to stop looking for things to do. Your journey has just begun because you now have the foundation for some even more exciting features, and they aren't very hard to configure either. The big hurdle is to know what you can do, and also how to get there.

This book is aimed to demystify some of the additional features within Dynamics AX that you may want to configure and start using, and will show you how to:

- Create configured products
- Improve costing analysis through costing sheets
- Use lean manufacturing processes to streamline productions
- Manage service jobs through service management
- Streamline the vendor onboarding process through the Vendor Portal
- Track vendor performance and scorecards
- Create retail stores and use POS registers

Building Dynamic Products with the Product Configurator

If you want to personalize your products a little, or if you are more of a configure to order operation where every product that you ship out the door is tailored to your customers specifications and needs then you will probably want to take advantage of the Product Configurator that is built into Dynamics AX. This feature allows you to create a product with a number of different attributes, and rules that will allow Dynamics AX to build a custom BOM every time the product is ordered, and also tell you if the product is even possible to make.

In this walkthrough we will show how to:

- Create A Constraint Based Product Master
- Create a Product Configuration Model
- Add Configuration Attributes
- Group Related Attributes
- Add Conditional Display Options
- Add Constraints to your Configuration Model
- Configure a BOMS Based On Attributes
- Use Table Based Attribute Values
- Use Attributes To Simplify Rules

Creating a Constraint Based Product Master

The first step in creating a Product Configuration is to create a **Product Master** that is enabled for **Constraint Based** configuration.

In this example we will show how to create a Constraint Based Product Master.

HOW TO DO IT...

Open the **Released Products** form from the **Common** group within the **Product information management** area page.

Click on the **Product** button in the **New** group on the **Product** ribbon bar.

In the **New Released product** quick creation form, change the **Product subtype** field to *Product master*.

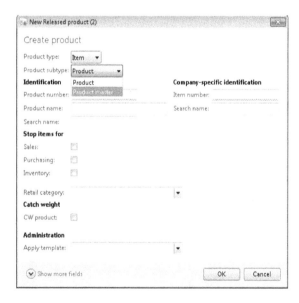

Give your product master a **Product number**, **Product name**, and also a **Search name**.

In order to the product to have product variants based on the configurations, we need to select the *Config* dimension group from the **Product dimension group** field.

From the **Configuration technology**, select the *Constraint-based configuration* value from the drop down list.

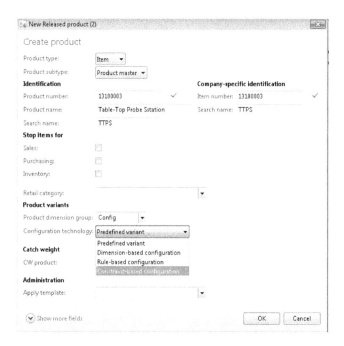

After filling in all of the other configurations that you want for the product, click on the **OK** button to complete the setup.

Creating a Product Configuration Model

Once you have a product to configure, it is time to create a Product Configuration Model. This is going to contain all of the rules and definitions that you will use to tell Dynamics AX how to build your new product BOM's.

In this example we will show how to create a new Product Configuration Model.

HOW TO DO IT...

To create a new product configuration model, follow these steps:

Open the Product configuration models form from the Common group within the Product information management area page.

To create a new model, click on the **Product configuration model** button in the **New** group of the **Model** ribbon bar.

Give your new configuration model a **Name**, **Description**, and also specify a new **Name** for the Root component.

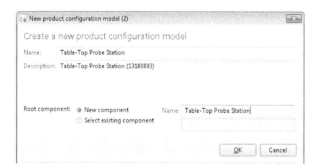

When the **Product configuration model** has been created, we need to link it to our product so that it will know to use it. To do this, click on the **Versions** button in the **Product model details** group of the **Models** ribbon bar.

Create a new version by clicking on the **New** menu button.

Specify the **Product number** that you want to associate with this configuration and enter a **From date** and **To date** for the model.

Tip: by default the model to and from dates will default in as today. In the **To date** field type in *12/32/2154* which is the AX date that equals Never.

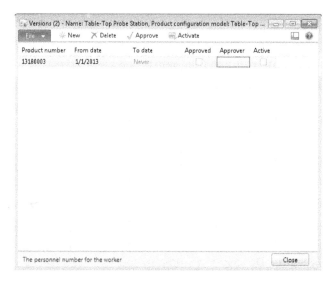

Once you have created the version, click on the **Approve** button in the menu bar.

When the **Approval** dialog box appears, select the **Approved By** user and click on the **OK** button.

Finally, click on the **Activate** menu button in the menu bar to allow the configuration version to be used.

Adding Configuration Attributes

The way that the configurations are personalized are though **Configuration Attributes** which the user will update as they are building their product variation.

In this example we will show how to create attributes and associate them with your product configuration.

HOW TO DO IT...

The first step is to create any new types of attributes that you may be using in this model. To do this, open the **Product configuration model** maintenance form and expand the **Attributes** panel. From the **Attributes** menu bar, click on the **Maintain attribute types** menu button.

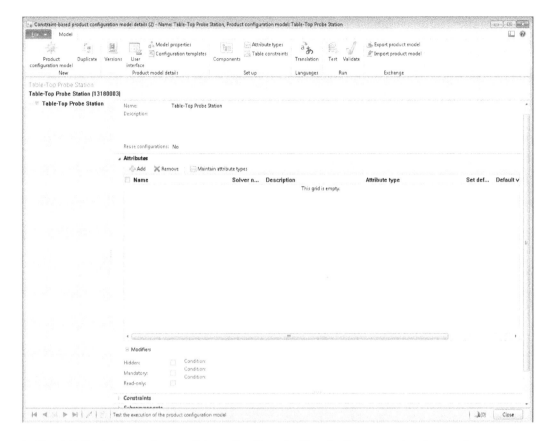

In the **Attribute types** form, click on the **New** button in the menu bar to create a new attribute type, and give it a **Name**.

Rather than having a free-text value that the user enters in, it's sometimes better to give them a list of valid configuration values that they can use in the **Attribute Type**. To do this, check the **Fixed list** check box.

Then click the **Add** button in the **Values** panel menu bar to add the valid values.

Tip: In these examples, we create the first entry as *None*. This allows you to have a null value that represents that the user has not selected anything yet.

Repeat the last step for every one of the valid configurations that you allow for the **Attribute type.**

When you have finished, click the **Close** button to return to the product configuration model.

Once we have an attribute type, we will create the **Attributes** that we will be using to describe our product. To do this, click on the **Add** menu item in the **Attributes** panel.

Give your attribute a **Name** which will be a friendly name for you.

Give it a **Solver name**. This is the variable name that you will use to reference it later on in your configuration rules.

Add a **Description** where you can add more detailed information about the attribute.

And then from the **Attribute** type drop down box, select the **Attribute type** that you just created which will be used as a template for this attribute.

Finally check the **Set default value** check box, and select one of the **Attribute values** from the **Default value** drop down box. We used the *None* value so that we will default it in as the unselected value.

HOW IT WORKS...

Now that we have configured an attribute, we can see it in action by clicking on the **Test** button in the **Run** group of the **Model** ribbon bar.

This will open up a configuration window, and we will see our attribute and be able to select form the drop down box the value that we want.

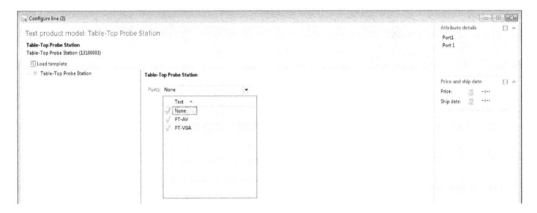

We can add more attributes exactly the same way. Note that in this example, we are creating six attributes that are similar, so we are reusing the same attribute type.

If we click the **Test** button again we will now see all of the other attributes that we created.

Grouping Related Attributes

If there are attributes that are related to each other then you may want to show them together in the configuration dialog box. To do this we need to change the way that they are displayed within the UI.

In this example we will show how you can group attributes together.

HOW TO DO IT...

Open the **Product configuration model** maintenance form and click on the **User interface** button in the **Product model details** group of the **Models** ribbon bar.

This will open up the **User interface** maintenance form. You can move the attributes around just by selecting them and clicking on the **Move up** and **Move down** menu items. But if you want to nest them together to make them stand out, then click on the **New attribute group** button in the menu bar.

Give your attribute group a new name, and then click on the **OK** button.

Now select the attribute that you want to move and select the group name from the **Attribute group** drop down list.

You can repeat this step for any other attributes you want to group.

After you have created all of your groupings, just click on the **Close** button.

Now that we have configured an attribute groups, we can see it in action by clicking on the **Test** button in the **Run** group of the **Model** ribbon bar. We will now see sections for each of the groupings that we created.

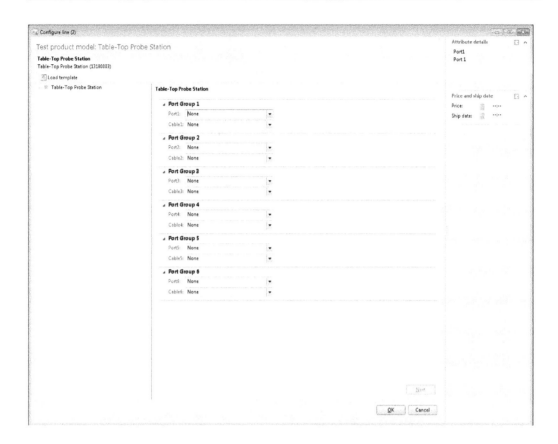

Adding Conditional Display Options

You may not want to show all of the attributes on the configuration screen initially. Some may be dependent on others being set, and others may have to be added sequentially so that you don't have gaps in the configuration attributes. You can do this through the product configurators conditional rules that allow you to show and hide attributes based on conditions.

In this example we will show how you can create conditional display rules on your attributes.

HOW TO DO IT...

Open the **Product configuration model** maintenance form and expand the **Attributes** panel. Select the **Attribute** that you want to add conditional display rules for.

To hide the attribute, check the **Hidden** check box.

To make the display conditional, add a rule in the **Condition** field.

Note: In this example, we are going to hide the *Port2* attribute when the value in *Port1* equals (==) *"None"*.

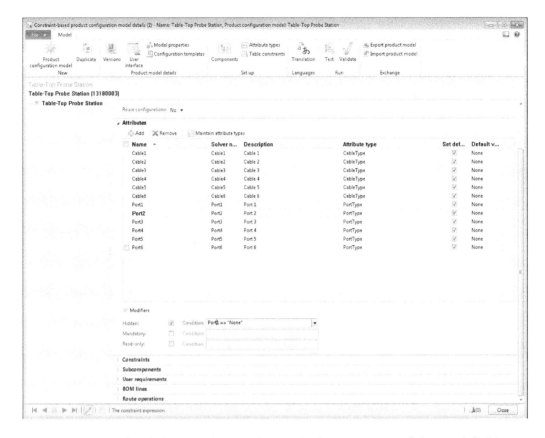

To see it in action by clicking on the **Test** button in the **Run** group of the **Model** ribbon bar. Notice that the *Port2* attribute is initially hidden.

When we select a value for the port then the *Port2* attribute is displayed.

We can add more conditional rules on when to hide and display the attributes. When we test the configuration display now, we don't see all of the other attributes initially. As we select the values, then only the new attribute options are shown.

Adding Constraints to your Configuration Model

You can further refine your **Product configuration model** by adding constraints. These are rules that allow you to restrict what values are allowed to be entered in the attributes based on the values of other attributes.

In this example we will show how you can add constraints to your configuration models.

HOW TO DO IT...

To create constraints, open the **Product configuration model** maintenance form and expand the **Constraints** panel. From the **Constraints** menu bar, click on the **Add** menu button.

When the new constraint dialog box is displayed, select the *Expression constraint* option from the **Constraint** drop down list. This will allow us to write a simple expression that defines what restrictions we are placing on the attribute.

Give your constraint a **Name**, and **Description**.

In the **Expression** field we will now write our rule that will tell Dynamics AX what is valid and what isn't, using the *Implies* function. The format is:

Implies[AttributeRuleIsImplied, WhenAttributeRuleIsTrue]

i.e. WhenAttributeRuleIsTrue (then) AttributeRuleIsImplied

Implies[Cable1 == "CT-AV1", Port1=="PT-AV"]

i.e. When Port1 is "AV" then Cable1 may be "CT-AV1"

Repeat the step and add as many constraints as you like.

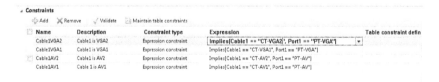

To see it in action by clicking on the **Test** button in the **Run** group of the **Model** ribbon bar. Notice that the attribute values that are not allowed are not checked, and also cannot be selected.

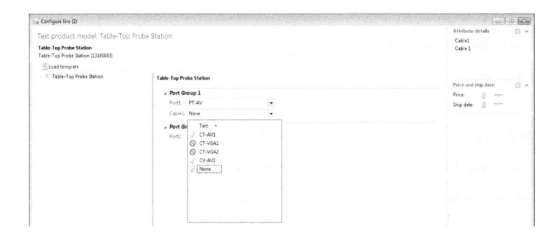

Configuring BOMS Based On Attributes

Once you have all of your attributes configured, with their values, and constraints, you can now create the rules that will allow Dynamics AX to use them to create dynamic BOM's on the fly.

In this example we will show how to define the rules for your Product model BOM's.

HOW TO DO IT...

Before we start though, make sure that you have created all of your product masters that you are going to be using in the BOM's that the Product configurator will be creating:

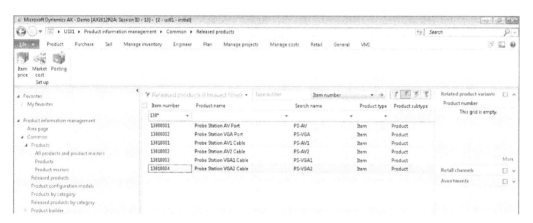

To define the BOM creation rules, open the **Product configuration model** maintenance form and expand the **BOM lines** panel. From the menu bar, click on the **Add** menu button to create a new BOM line rule.

Give your **BOM line** rule a unique **Name** and a **Description**.

If this BOM line is dependent on an attribute being a certain value then add the expression that you want to check in the **Condition** field.

Once you have created the line, click on eth **BOM details** button in the **BOM lines** menu bar to open the BOM line designer.

In the **BOM line details** form, enter in the **Item number** that you want to use in the **BOM line**.

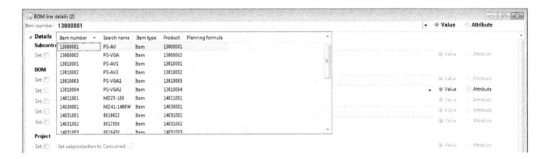

Then configure any of the BOM line fields that you want to use. In this example we set the **Calculation**, **Quantity**, and **Unit** fields.

Continue this for all of the other types of BOM lines that you want Dynamics AX to use.

Tip: after creating all of your rules, click on the **Validate** button in the **Run** group of the **Models** ribbon bar to check all of your conditions, and expressions. If there are any errors then it will notify you and you can debug your rules.

To see this in action, you can create a new sales order and create a line on the order for the configured product that you just created. Open up the detail tabs at the bottom, and select the **Products** tab. Notice that there is no **Sub-BOM** value at this point.

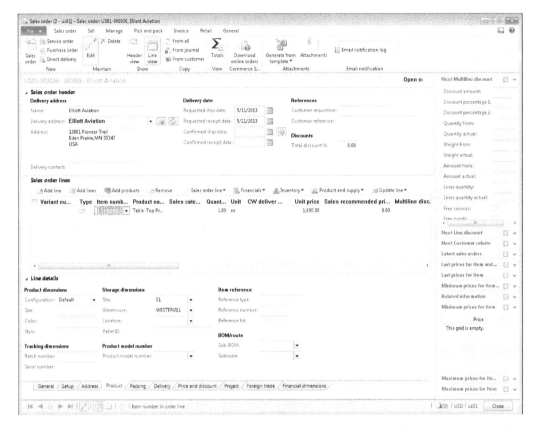

From the **Product and supply** drop down menu in the **Sales order lines** panel, select the **Configure line** menu item.

This will open up the same configuration screen that you have seen during the testing of your product configuration. Fill in the attributes that you want to use for the product configuration, and click the **OK** button.

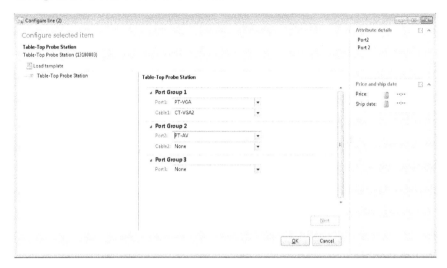

After you have finished, you will now see that Dynamics AX has created and assigned a **Sub-BOM** to your order line.

If you drill into the Sub-BOM you will see that it has created a new BOM, you will see the BOM lines that it has automatically built for you.

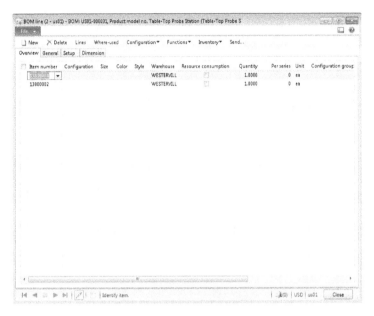

Additionally, from the **Update line** drop down menu in the **Sales order lines** panel, select the **(Calculate) Based on BOM/Formula** menu item.

This will open up the cost calculation form for quotation purposes. To calculate the cost of the product configuration, just click on the **OK** button. You will then be shown how much the configuration will cost to build based on the base components of the BOM allowing you to quote the expected price to the customer.

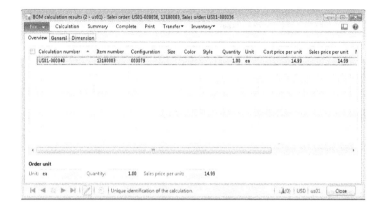

Using Table Based Attribute Values

You don't have to hard code the attribute values as we have done in the previous examples. The Product configurator has the ability to look up the values directly from the database, allowing you to dynamically update attribute values.

In this example we will show how to create Attribute values based on live table data.

HOW TO DO IT...

To do this, open the **Product configuration model** maintenance form, expand the **Attributes** panel, and click on the **Maintain table constraints** button in the **Attributes** menu bar.

When the **Table constraints** maintenance form appears, click on the **New** button in the menu bar.

This will start off the **New table constraint** wizard. Click **Next** through the introduction screen.

Give your table constraint a **Name**, and **Description**, and then change the **Type** to **System Defined**.

This will allow you to then choose a table from the **Select table** drop down box.

When you have finished, click the **Next** button.

In the next wizard step, click on the **Add** button to add attribute values to our table constraint.

Select the fields that you want to pick from the table within Dynamics AX, and link them to the **Attribute type**.

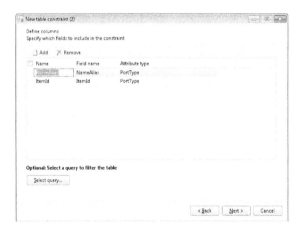

Once you have defined your attributes, click on the **Select query** button to add a filter to the returned values.

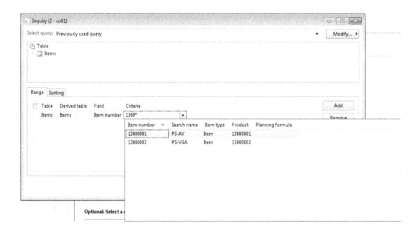

In the Select query, add a wildcard filter onto the table that you are querying, and then click on the **OK** button to return to the wizard, and then click the **Next** button to continue on.

To complete the process, click on the **Finish** button on the wizard.

Repeat this step for any other tables that you want to add constraints based on table data.

To use the **Table constraints,** create a new **Constraint** by clicking on the **Add** button in the **Constraints** menu bar.

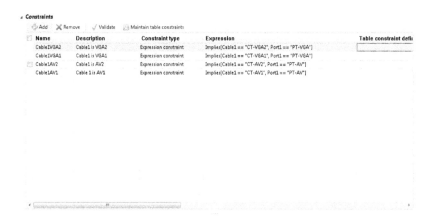

Rather than using the *Expression constraint* as we have done in the previous examples, this time change the **Constraint** to *Table constraint*, and click the **Create** button.

Give your new constraint a **Name**, **Description** and then click the drop down button in the **Table constraint definition** field.

This will open up the **Table constraint attachment** form. In the **Table constraint name** field, select the attribute type that you want to override the drop down list on.

Then select the attribute that you want to use from the attribute tree and select the column that you want to use for its lookup from the **Table constraint column** dropdown box.

When you have finished, click the **Close** button.

Repeat this process for any additional attributes that you want to link to the table constraints.

Tip: One thing that you may want to do though it to add additional dummy configuration fields into Dynamics AX for the null values. This will allow you to have the unselected option show up when the configuration screen is displayed.

Now when you test the **Product configuration model**, the data that is listed against the attributes is being pulled from the database.

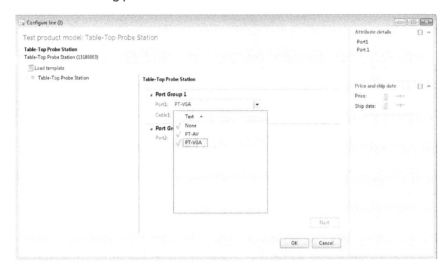

If we add a new record to the database that matches the selection criteria within the constraint, then it will automatically be shown in the configuration screen.

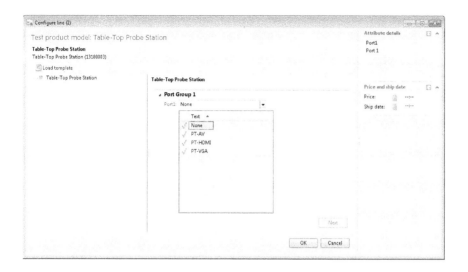

Using Attributes as Variables

Attributes do not have to be values that the user enters. They can also be used to store related information that you can then use within the constraints and rules of the Product configuration model. This allows you to simplify your models, and also makes them more flexible as well.

In this example we will show how you can use attributes as variables within your configuration model.

HOW TO DO IT...

First, open the **Product configuration model** maintenance form, expand the **Attributes** panel, and click on the **New** button to create a new attribute.

Note: in this example we are creating an attribute for the ItemId that will be linked to the selections that are made within the other attributes. We didn't bother setting a default value.

Check the **Read only** check box in the **Modifiers** group. This makes sure that the value is only changed by the system.

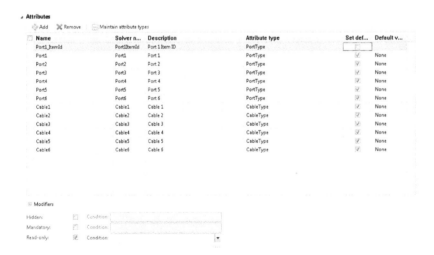

Then open up the **Constraints** panel, and select the **Table constraint definition** dropdown for the attribute that you want to link to the attribute.

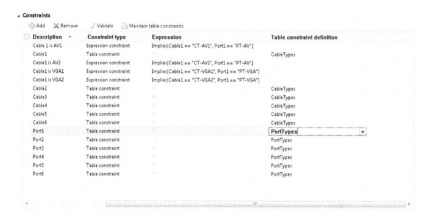

In the **Table constraint attachment** form, add an additional column constraint, but this time, link the *ItemId* to the new attribute that we just created. This will populate the attribute with the corresponding Id linked to the *NameAlias* of the product.

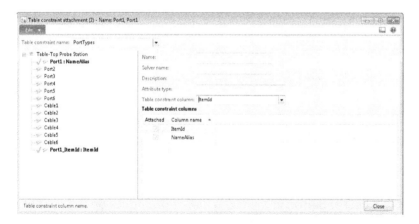

To see this in action click the **Test** button. Notice that the Attributes are already populated. When the attribute value is changed, then the other reference attribute changes as well.

As an example of how to use the attribute, we will use it to simplify the **BOM lines** rules. We will delete all but one of the lines for the associated attribute, change the **Name**, and **Description**, and then change the **Condition** to *Port1 != (is not equal to) "None"*.

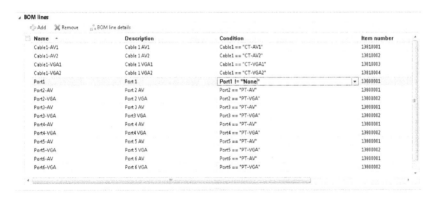

Then click on the **BOM line details** button in the menu bar. If you notice on the right of the **BOM line details** there are radio boxes for **Value** and **Attribute**. Up until now we have just been hard coding values. If we change the selection to **Attribute** then we can select any of the attributes and use the current value in there as the value for that element. Select your reference attribute, and then click the **OK** button.

Now you will see that the **Item number** field is being populated from an attribute.

Tip: After you create the reference attribute, you may want to check the **Hidden** check box on the attribute so that it doesn't show on the configuration form.

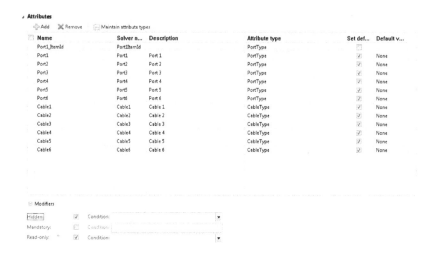

If you repeat this process on all of the other BOM lines that are configured based on the attribute values, then your **BOM lines** will look a lot tidier.

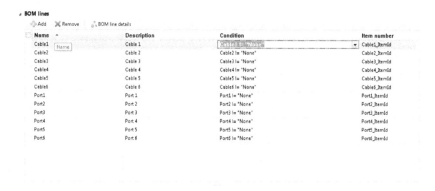

Tip: You may also want to update your User Interface configuration as well and group your variables with your display attributes... just to be tidy.

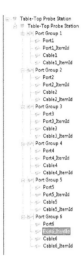

Now when you configure your order line, it will be built from the data within your product tables.

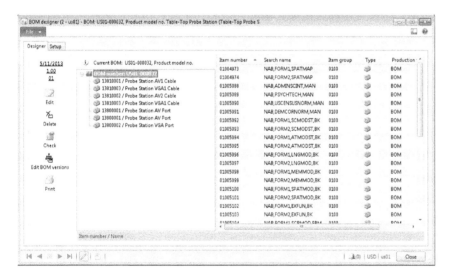

Summary

The Product Configurator that is built into Dynamics AX is a pretty useful tool, and if you spend the time creating the rules on how you should be building your products, it can possibly reduce the number of BOM's that you define down to just a handful.

Configuring Costing & Cost Sheets

If you are using the production module within Dynamics AX, then you are probably wanting to get a better handle on your costs. You can easily configure Dynamics AX to calculate costs of BOM's, and if you want to get a little more industrious then you can also create cost sheets broken out by your particular cost categories, incorporate routing costs, and even add surcharges and other indirect costs.

In this example we will walk through an example that shows how to set up your costing controls within Dynamics AX. You will learn how to:

- Set up Costing Versions
- Manually assign a Product Cost
- Create Calculation Groups
- Use Costing Versions to perform a mass cost calculation
- Perform a basic Cost Rollup
- Create Cost Groups
- Build a Costing Sheet
- Define Route Shared Categories
- Define Route Cost Categories
- Add Surcharges and Fixed Overhead Costs

Setting up Costing Versions

Costing Versions are used within Dynamics AX to store the costs of your products, and are also used by the BOM cost calculations as reference costs. You can have as many costing versions as you like and can separate them out as Standard, and Planned versions. You can use them to track historical costs, actual production costs, and also financial costs used for analysis.

In this example we will show how you can create a new Costing Version.

HOW TO DO IT...

To access the costing versions, select the **Costing versions** menu item from the **Costing** folder in the **Setup** group of the **Inventory and warehouse management** area page.

When the **Costing versions** maintenance form is displayed, click on the **New** button in the menu bar to create a new record.

From the **Costing type** drop down, select the *Standard cost* option.

Assign a **Version** and **Name** to your new Costing Version.

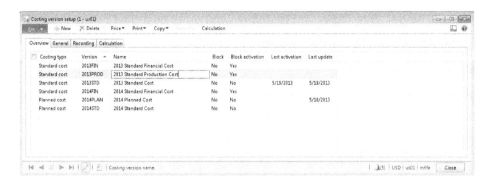

Tip: If you want to use this Costing version within other cost roll ups, then you may want to set the **Block activation** field to *No*.

Tip: If you access the **Recording** tab on the Costing Version form, you can define a default **Site** and also turn on or off the ability to use the Costing Version for Purchasing, Costing, and Sales. In this example we will just allow it to be used for Costing.

Tip: Also, if you access the **Calculation** tab on the Costing Version form, you can define a

Fallback principle model. This allows you to define what other cost the Costing Version will use if there is no explicit cost defined against the product.

When you have finished, click on the **Close** button to exit the form.

Manually Assigning a Product Cost

Every product that you are using should have a cost defined against it.

In this example we will show how you can manually assign a cost to your Released Products within Dynamics AX.

HOW TO DO IT...

To update your product costs, open up the **Released products** form from within the **Common** group of the **Product information management** area page.

Select the product that you want to assign the cost to, and then select the **Item price** menu button from the **Set up** group of the **Manage Costs** ribbon bar.

When the **Item Price** form is displayed, click on the **Ned** button in the menu bar to create a new record.

From the **Price type** dropdown, select the *Cost* option.

Note: you can also assign the Purchase and Sales prices here as well.

Now select your **Costing Version** that you want to assign the cost to.

If you have defined a default site for your costing version then you will not need to enter that here. All you need to do is enter the cost that you want to assign to the product in the **Price unit** field.

Note: If you want, you can change the default **From date** to a later date.

Once you have saved your record, you can click on the **Activate** button in the menu bar.

If you switch to the **Active prices** tab on the form you will be able to see all of the Costs and Prices that have been defined for your product.

You can now click the **Close** button to exit out of the form.

Creating Calculation Groups

Calculation groups are used to define how costs are calculated for individual products and also how costs are modeled based on other price and cost elements within Dynamics AX.

In this example we will show how to create a cost calculation group that will use the default purchase price as the basis.

HOW TO DO IT...

Open the **Calculation groups** menu item from the **Costing** folder in the **Setup** group of the **Inventory and warehouse management** area page.

When the **Calculation groups** maintenance form opens, click on the **New** button on the menu bar.

Enter a code in the **Calculation group** field and a description in the **Name** field.

From the **Cost price model** dropdown, select the *Item purchase price* option to use the default purchase price when calculating default costs.

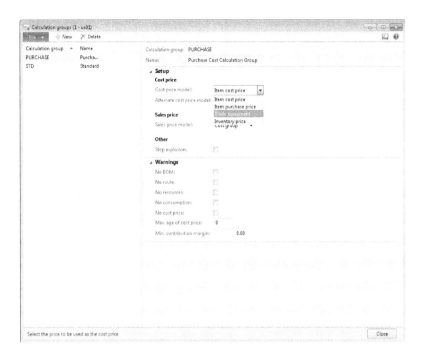

When you have finished, click on the **Close** button to exit the form.

Now open up your **Released product details** and within the **Engineer** group you can select your new **Calculation Group**.

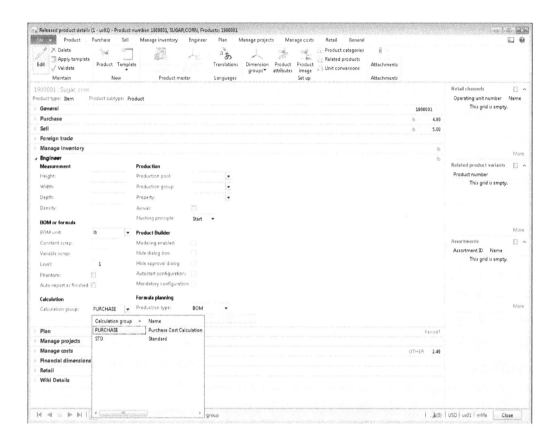

Using Costing Versions to perform a Mass Cost Calculation

Once you have defined **Calculation groups** to your products, you can take advantage of them by performing mass updates of your costs through the **Costing versions**. This saves you a lot of time, and also makes the cost maintenance so much easier.

In this example we will show how to perform a mass cost calculation.

HOW TO DO IT...

Select the **Costing versions** menu item from the **Costing** folder in the **Setup** group of the **Inventory and warehouse management** area page.

Select the **Costing version** that you want to create your costs for and then click on the **Calculation** menu item that is in the menu bar.

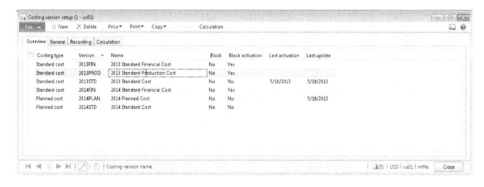

This will open up the cost calculation form. You can update all of your product costs just by clicking the **OK** button.

Tip: If you just want to update a subset of your products, then you can change the selection filter by clicking on the **Select** button to the right of the form. In this example we added a new filter field for the **Calculation group** and selected just the items that are purchased.

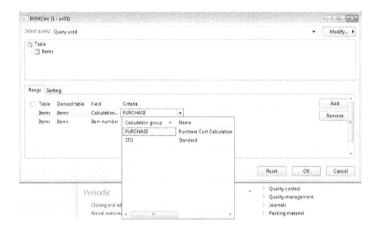

Once the update has run, you can see all of the prices by selecting the **Item price** menu item from the **Price** menu group. This will show you all of the costs that are associated with your **Costing version**.

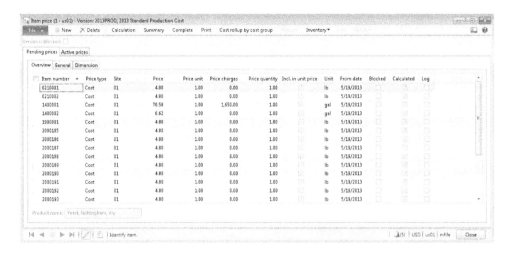

Also, if you look at your products within the **Released products** form, and select the **Item price** menu item from the **Setup** group of the **Manage costs** ribbon bar, you will be able to see the Cost version details.

Performing a Basic Cost Rollup

Once all of your base products have costs associated to them, you can use them to calculate your rolled up BOM costs.

In this example we will show how to roll up your BOM costs.

HOW TO DO IT...

Open up the **Released products** form from within the **Common** group of the **Product information management** area page.

There are a couple of different ways to perform a cost roll up. You can access it through the BOM Designer view and also from the Item Prices forms. To do it the first way, select the product that you want to perform the cost roll up on, and then click on the **Designer** menu item in the **Formula** or **BOM** groups of the **Engineer** ribbon bar.

When the **Designer** shows up, click on the **Calculation** button on the left hand side.

This will open up the **BOM or formula calculation** form. Select the Costing version that you want to use as the basis for your cost roll up, and then click the **OK** button.

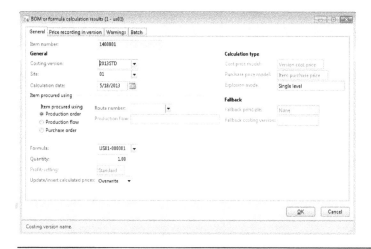

After the cost roll up has been performed, you will see a list of all of the pending prices that have been calculated.

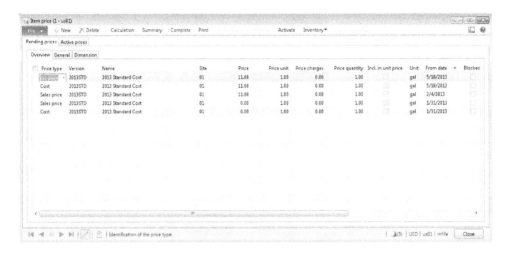

Note: you can get to the same screens by selecting the **Item prices** menu item from the **Set up** group of the **Manage costs** ribbon bar. To perform a calculation, just click on the **Calculation** button in the menu bar.

Creating Cost Groups

You can start to break down your costs into a more granular level by assigning Cost Groups to your products. This allows the costing to lump costs together into costing buckets so that you can see them by product group, or type of product. This will also allow you to track costing changes by the costing groups.

In this example we will show how you can create and use **Cost Groups**.

HOW TO DO IT...

Open up the **Cost groups** form from within the **Costing** folder of the **Setup** group of the **Inventory and warehouse management** area page.

Click on the **New** menu button to create a new **Cost group** record.

In this example we will create cost groups for each of the types of ingredients that we are using in our BOM/Formula. Start off by assigning a **Cost group** code, and a **Name**.

From the **Cost group type** drop down, select the *Direct materials* option since these are all going to be assigned to ingredients.

In the **Behavior** field, select the *Variable cost* option.

Repeat this process for all of the other **Cost groups** that you want to use, and then click the **Close** button to finish the setup.

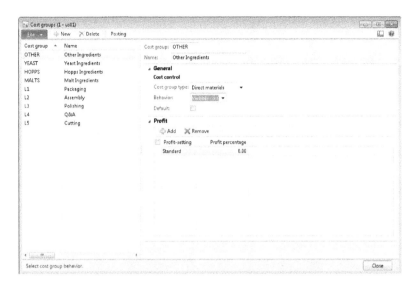

To use the **Cost groups** open up your **Released product** records that you are using in your BOM, and update the **Cost group** field in the **Manage costs** group to reflect the cost group that you want to use.

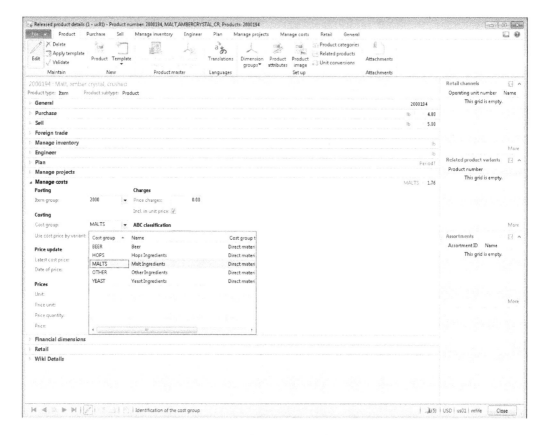

Now, when you re-run the cost roll up for your BOM/Formula, if you click on the **Cost rollup by cost group** menu item within the **Item price** maintenance form, you will see a breakdown of your costs by cost group.

Building a Costing Sheet Template

You can improve the way that the costs are being summarized by creating a **Costing Sheet**. This allows you to add additional hierarchies to your costing so that you can group cost groups, and also add summary totals at any level you like.

In this example we will show how to build a simple Cost Sheet.

HOW TO DO IT...

Open up the **Costing Sheets** form from within the **Costing** folder of the **Setup** group of the **Inventory and warehouse management** area page.

When the Costing Sheet form is displayed, if this is the first time that you have accessed the **Costing sheet** you should just see the **Root** node.

To start building your Costing Sheet, right-mouse-click on the Root node, and select **Create** from the context menu.

Change the **Type** from Undefined to Cost of goods manufactured.

Change the **Description** to something that makes a little more sense.

Then check both the **Header** and **Total** check boxes – this will add header information and also a total of the costs at this level.

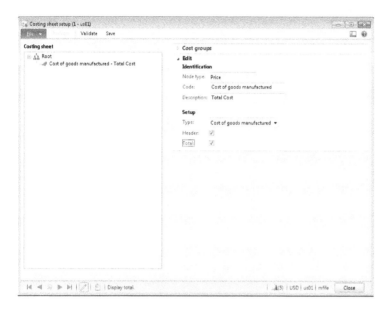

Now we want to create groups for the different types of costs that we can have within our Costing Sheet. To do this, right-mouse-click on the new Cost node that we just created and select the **Create** submenu item again.

When the **Create new node** dialog box pops up, we will need to choose the type of node that we want to create. Select the *Total* option and then click the **OK** button.

Give your node a **Code** and **Description.**

Also, so that we see the group and the totals, check both the **Header**, and **Totals** check boxes.

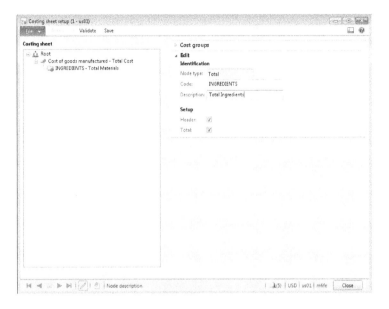

Repeat this process for all of the other Cost Groups that you want to show in your Costing sheet.

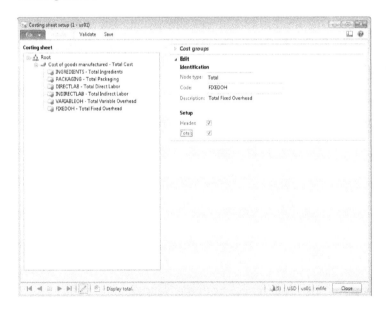

Now we want to add our **Cost Groups** to the **Costing Sheet**. To do this, right-mouse-click on the node that you want to add the Cost Group to and select the **Create** option.

This time, select the **Node type** of *Cost group*.

After giving your node a **Name**, and **Description**, you will also be able to select the **Cost group**.

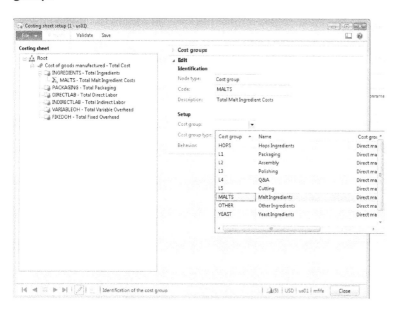

Repeat this step for each of the other Cost Groups.

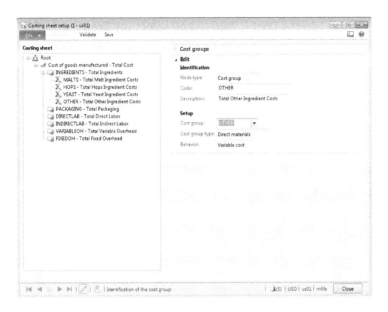

To see the cost groups and costing sheet in action, open up the **Item price** form, and click on the **Complete** menu item. This will show you all of the individual costs by ingredient for your BOM/Formula.

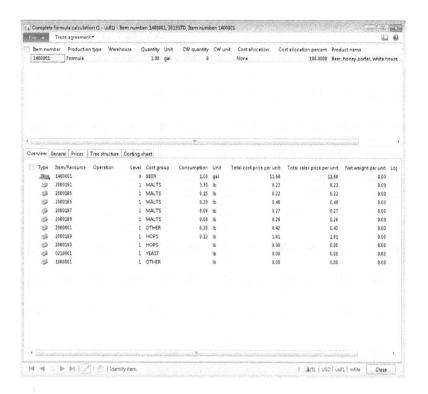

You can see the costs in the **Costing Sheet** format, just click on the **Costing sheet** tab.

Up until now, we have just been looking at the planned costs of the products. All of the cost structures that we have been configuring will be available for analyzing the execution of the production orders as well.

If you open up your **Production orders** you can see the cost break down by clicking on the **Price calculation** button within the **Related information** group of the **View** ribbon bar.

If you select the **Overview costing** tab, you will see all of the estimated and actual consumption.

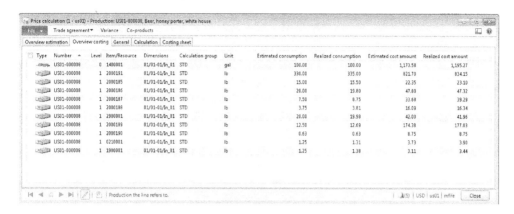

Clicking on the **Costing sheet** tab will show you the cost break down in the format that you defined in the **Costing sheet** setup.

Also, clicking on the **Variance** menu item will show you any variances between the estimates, and actual consumption.

Defining Route Shared Categories

In addition to costing by the BOM/Formula, you can model your **Routing** costs as well and capture labor, and machine overhead costs. To start this setup we need to create some Shared Categories that we will be able to associate with the route cost categories.

In this example we will show how to create **Route Shared Categories**.

HOW TO DO IT...

Open up the **Shared categories** form from within the **Routes** folder of the **Setup** group of the **Production control** area page.

To create a new **Shared category**, click on the **New** button in the menu bar.

Give your Shared category a Category ID, Category name and then check the Can be used in Production check box.

Repeat the process for each of the Shared categories that you want track costs by.

Note: In this example we created **Shared categories** for each of the steps within the route, and also each step has three variations (PROC, QTY, & SETUP) so that we can capture different categories by stage in the Route.

Defining Route Cost Categories

Once you have created **Shared categories** you want to associate them to Route **Cost Categories** so that we can assign them to a Route.

In this example we will show how to create Route **Cost Categories**.

HOW TO DO IT...

Open up the **Cost categories** form from within the **Routes** folder of the **Setup** group of the **Production control** area page.

Click on the **New** menu button to create a new **Cost category**.

From the **Category ID** drop sown, select one of the **Shared Categories** that were created in the previous step.

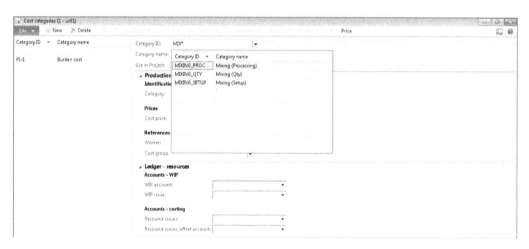

In the **Reference** group, assign a **Cost group** to the **Cost** Category, and then define the Ledger accounts in the **Ledger** group.

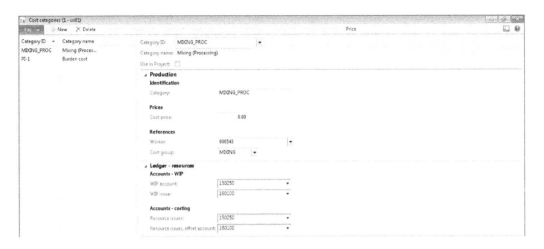

Note: When you create the **Cost Groups** for these **Cost Categories** set the **Cost Group Type** to *Direct manufacturing*.

Then click on the **Price** menu item to open up the **Cost category prices** form. Assign your **Cost Category** a Price that reflects the cost per hour.

To make the price active, click on the **Activate** button in the menu bar, and then click **Close** to finish the update.

Note: The reason why we have broken out our **Cost Categories** into Processing, Qty, and Setup is because we may want to have different resources associated with the operations that have different costs. i.e. Setup may require an expert resources, whereas the operation may just require a general worker, thus having different costs associated to them for the costing to take into account.

Repeat this process for all of the cost categories and then click the **Close** button.

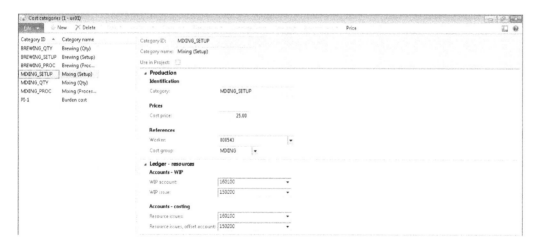

HOW IT WORKS...

Once the Cost Categories have been defined, you can associate them to your Route steps by opening up your Route, and selecting the **Setup** tab for each of the lines. You will see the three buckets for the **Cost Categories** that you can associate with the appropriate **Cost Categories** that you just created.

Return to your **Costing Sheet** template, and add the Direct Manufacturing operations.

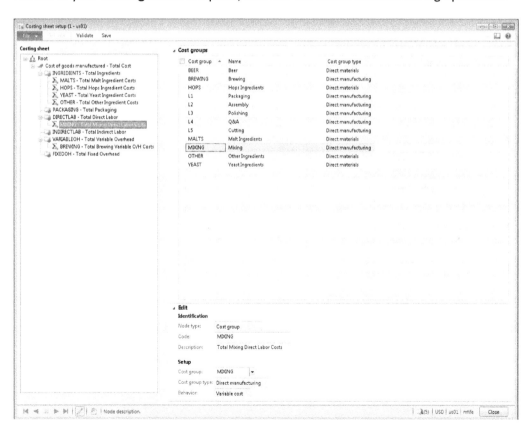

Tip: In this example we just expanded out the **Cost groups** and dragged them over to the **Costing Sheet**.

Now when you perform a cost roll up of your BOM/Formula, you will notice more costs being added to the cost Overview.

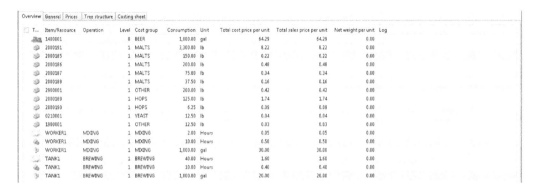

If you look at the **Costing sheet** you will see the **Direct manufacturing** operations being shown there as well.

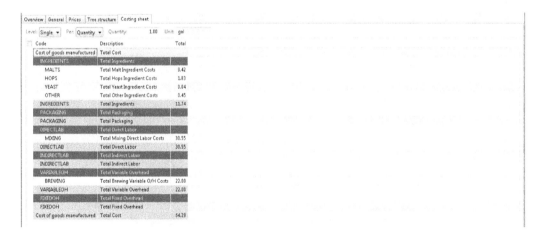

Tip: If you change the **Quantity** at the top of the **Costing sheet** tab, the costs will scale.

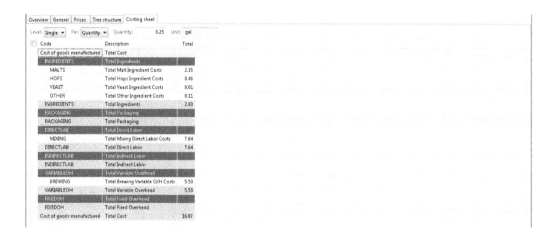

Code	Description	Total
Cost of goods manufactured	Total Cost	
INGREDIENTS	Total Ingredients	
MALTS	Total Malt Ingredient Costs	2.35
HOPS	Total Hops Ingredient Costs	0.46
YEAST	Total Yeast Ingredient Costs	0.01
OTHER	Total Other Ingredient Costs	0.11
INGREDIENTS	Total Ingredients	2.93
PACKAGING	Total Packaging	
PACKAGING	Total Packaging	
DIRECTLAB	Total Direct Labor	
MIXING	Total Mixing Direct Labor Costs	7.64
DIRECTLAB	Total Direct Labor	7.64
INDIRECTLAB	Total Indirect Labor	
INDIRECTLAB	Total Indirect Labor	
VARIABLEOH	Total Variable Overhead	
BREWING	Total Brewing Variable O/H Costs	5.50
VARIABLEOH	Total Variable Overhead	5.50
FIXEDOH	Total Fixed Overhead	
FIXEDOH	Total Fixed Overhead	
Cost of goods manufactured	Total Cost	16.07

Adding Surcharges and Fixed Overheads

You can incorporate Surcharges and Overhead costs into your costing calculations. These could be used to recover costs based on variability of material costs, or could be used to capture per piece production costs that are not being captured within the BOM/Formula or Route.

In this example we will show how to add Surcharges to your Costing Sheets.

HOW TO DO IT...

Before you start, make sure that you have a **Costing group** defined with a **Cost group type** of *Indirect*, and a **Behavior** of *Fixed cost*.

Open up your **Costing sheet** and add your Indirect **Cost Groups**.

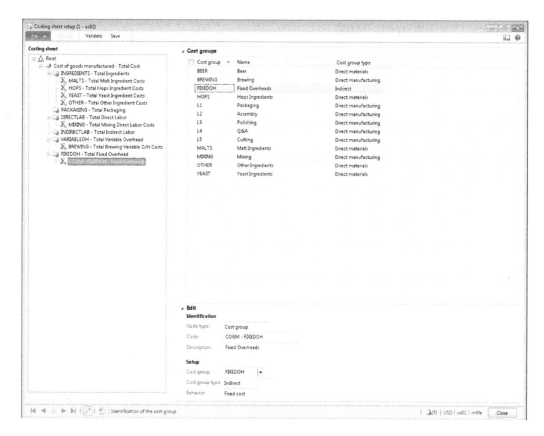

Now you want to create a new node attached to the Indirect cost node. To do this, right-mouse-click on the node, and select the **Create** option.

For this node type, you will notice that there are a lot more Node types available for selection.

Select the *Surcharge* option from the **Select node type** drop down box and click **OK**.

Select the new *Surcharge* node and give it a more appropriate **Code** and **Description**.

Also, change the **Subtype** to *Total*.

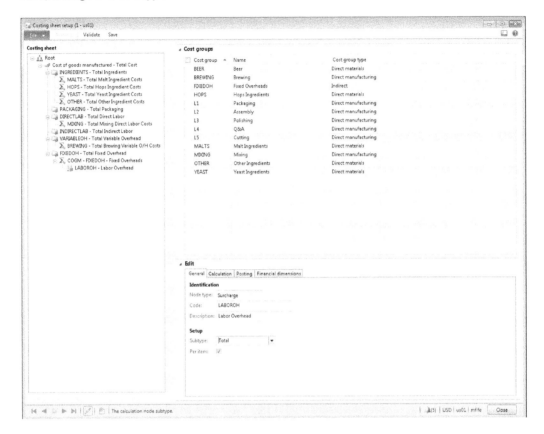

Note: If you want to add a surcharge for every item that is produced, you can check the **Per item** check box.

Now select the **Calculation** tab, and select the **Code** from the **Costing sheet** that you want to calculate the surcharge on.

Then in the **Surcharge** panel that shows up at the bottom of the form, select the **Percentage** that you want to apply to the surcharge.

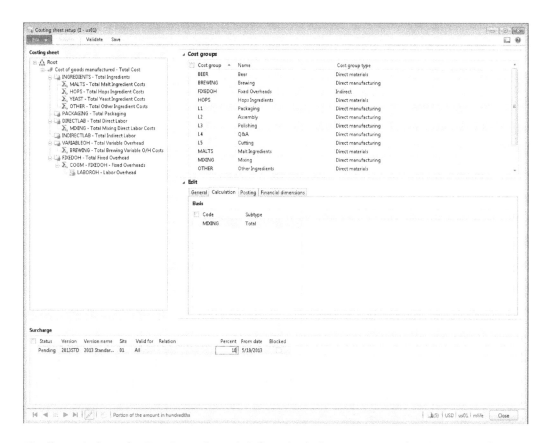

Finally, switch to the **Posting** tab, and define the ledger accounts that you want the Surcharge to post to.

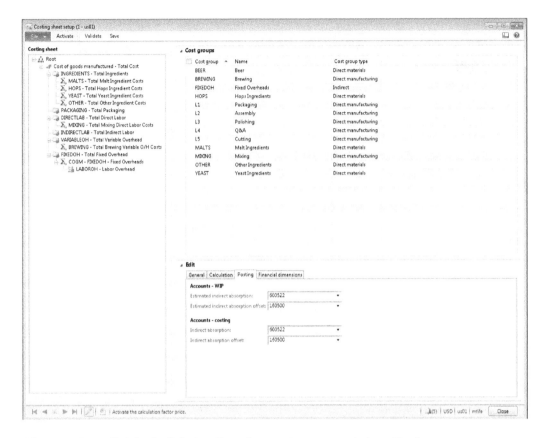

After you have finished, click the **Close** button to save and close the form.

Now when you perform a cost calculation roll up, you will see an additional Surcharge line being calculated.

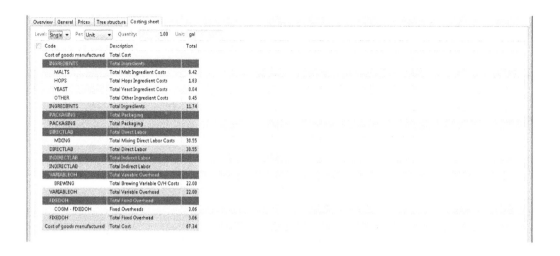

Level: Single ▼	Per: Unit ▼	Quantity:	1.00	Unit: gal
Code	Description	Total		
Cost of goods manufactured	Total Cost			
INGREDIENTS	Total Ingredients			
MALTS	Total Malt Ingredient Costs	9.42		
HOPS	Total Hops Ingredient Costs	1.83		
YEAST	Total Yeast Ingredient Costs	0.04		
OTHER	Total Other Ingredient Costs	0.45		
INGREDIENTS	Total Ingredients	11.74		
PACKAGING	Total Packaging			
PACKAGING	Total Packaging			
DIRECTLAB	Total Direct Labor			
MIXING	Total Mixing Direct Labor Costs	30.55		
DIRECTLAB	Total Direct Labor	30.55		
INDIRECTLAB	Total Indirect Labor			
INDIRECTLAB	Total Indirect Labor			
VARIABLEOH	Total Variable Overhead			
BREWING	Total Brewing Variable O/H Costs	22.00		
VARIABLEOH	Total Variable Overhead	22.00		
FIXEDOH	Total Fixed Overhead			
COGM - FIXEDOH	Fixed Overheads	3.06		
FIXEDOH	Total Fixed Overhead	3.06		
Cost of goods manufactured	Total Cost	67.34		

Summary

There is a lot more that you can do within the Costing configuration of Dynamics AX that we did not cover in this brief introduction. Try it out and I'm sure that you will quickly surpass what we did here.

Configuring Lean Manufacturing

This week I have been working with the Lean Manufacturing capabilities within Dynamics AX 2012, and had the opportunity to set up a number of different examples of how the Lean Manufacturing functions. I have to admit, I think this is very cool, and is pretty easy to set up.

In this worked example I will show you how you can create a simple set of Lean Manufacturing processes and see them in in action.

Configuring a Value Stream

There are a couple of codes that need to be configured before we can start building our Lean Manufacturing processes. The first is a Value Stream, which allows you to segregate out your Lean Manufacturing processes.

HOW TO DO IT...

From the **Production Control** area page, select the **Value streams** menu item from the **Organization** folder within the **Setup** group.

When the **Value Stream** maintenance form opens up, click on the **New** button to create a new Value Stream.

All you need to fill out in the Value Stream is the **Name** and the **Search Name** fields.

After you have done that, click the **Close** button to finish.

Configuring a Production Group

The next code that needs to be configured is the **Production Group**. These configure the default GL posting profiles for your production flows.

HOW TO DO IT...

From the **Production Control** area page, select the **Production groups** menu item from the **Production** folder of the **Setup** group.

When the **Production groups** maintenance form opens up, click on the **New** button to create a new record.

In the new record, specify the **Production group** and the **Name**. We will not need to configure the default prosing profiles at this point.

When you have finished doing this, click the **Close** button to exit out of the form.

Creating a Production Flow Model

Finally, we need to create a new **Production Flow Model** for our example. This will define the default options for our **Production Flows** and will be used by Dynamics AX to define how the Production Flows are planned.

HOW TO DO IT...

From the **Production Control** area page, select the **Production flow models** menu item from the **Lean Manufacturing** folder of the **Setup** group.

When the **Production flow** maintenance form is displayed, click on the **New** button in the menu bar to create a new record.

Enter a name into the **Production flow model** field.

In the **Model type** field, select the *Throughput* option.

Within the **Kanban schedule** group, select the option that you want to use in the **Cpacity shortage reaction** field. In this example we chose *Postpone*.

Within the **Planning period type** select the time interval for planning. In this example we will plan daily.

Then specify the **Planning time fence** value.

Finally, set the **EPE Cycle in days** to *1*.

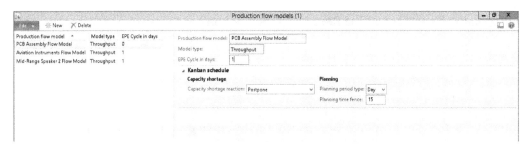

Once you have set up the **Production flow model** click the **Close** button to exit out of the form.

Creating a Work Cell

Now that we have the Lean Manufacturing codes defined, we can start defining our work cells. These are just the normal **Resource Groups** that are used in the traditional manufacturing models, except we configure a few additional pieces of information required for the Lean Manufacturing process.

HOW TO DO IT...

From the **Organization Administration** area page, select the **Resource groups** menu item from the **Resources** folder of the **Common** group.

When the **Resource groups** maintenance form opens, click on eth **Resource Group** button in the **New** group of the **Resource group** ribbon bar to create a new record.

Enter a code for your **Resource Group** into the **Resource group** field, and a description of the resource group into the **Description** field.

Also select the main site for the **Resource Group** from the **Site** drop down box.

Check the **Work cell** box within the **General** tab to turn the allow it to be used by Lean Manufacturing as a work cell.

Within the **Locations** group of the **General** tab, add the Input and Output warehouse and location for the work cell.

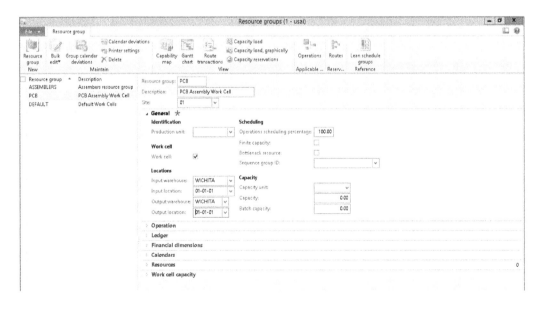

Expand the **Calendars** tab on the form, and click on the **Add** button.

Then select a calendar for the work cell to operate on.

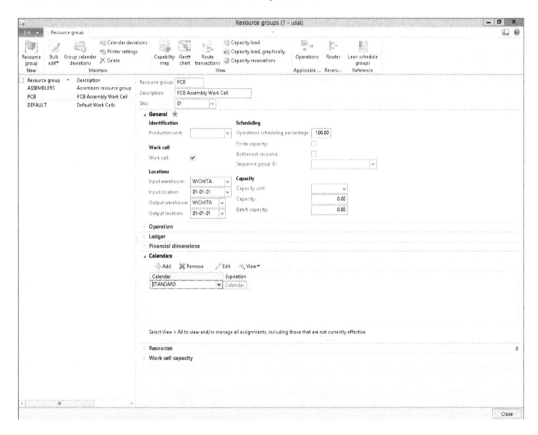

One thing to check is that on the **Calendar** that you are using, make sure that there is a value in the **Standard work day hours** field. If you don't have a value here, then you will grind to a halt later on in the process.

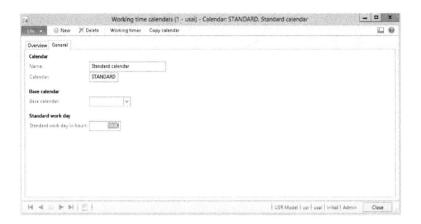

Finally, open up the **Work cell capacity** tab within the **Resource Group** and click the **Add** button to add a new record.

Select the **Production flow model** that was set up earlier on in the process.

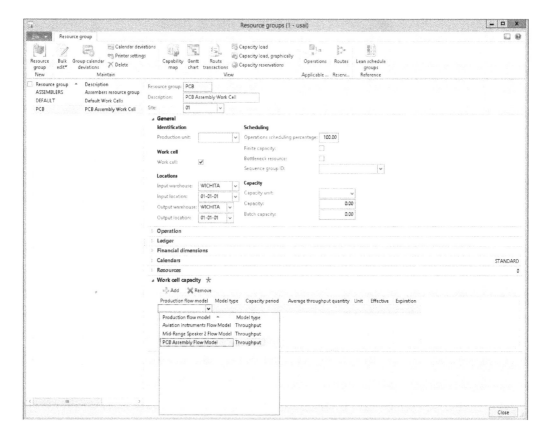

Select the **Capacity period** that you want to use for the work cell. In this case, we will use the *Standard work day.*

Then define the Average throughput and unit for the work cell.

Once you have set an **Effictive date** for the Production flow model, click the **Close** button to exit out of the form.

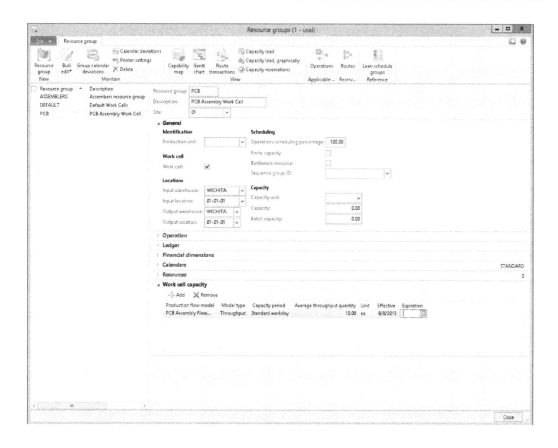

Creating a Production Flow

Now we will need to set up a new **Production Flow** for our Lean Manufacturing process. The **Production Flows** are the Lean equivalent of a production route, and will allow you to group lean activities together.

HOW TO DO IT...

From the **Production control** area page, select the **Production flows** menu item from the **Lean Manufacturing** folder of the **Setup** group.

When the **Production flow** form appears, click on the **New** button in the menu bar to create a new record.

Enter a name for the Production Flow into the **Name** field, and a short description into the **Description** field.

Then enter assign the **Value stream** and the **Production group** that we created in the earlier steps to the **Production flow**.

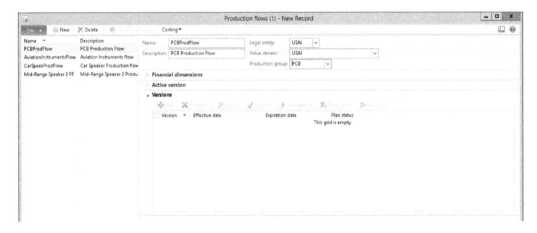

Open up the **Versions** tab, and click on the **Add** button to create a new version record.

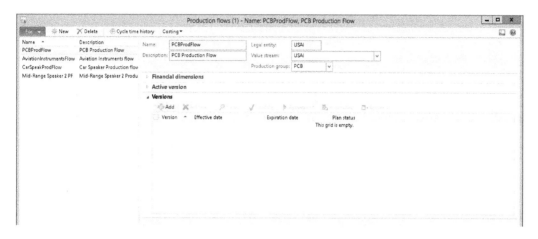

When the dialog box appears, enter a value into the **Effective date** field, and then click the **OK** button.

Now you will have a version record for the **Production flow**. You will not be able to activate it just yet though, because you need to assign activities to the Production Flow.

Creating a Production Flow Activity

Once we have a **Production Flow** record we need to define the activities that will be performed within that flow. These include production steps and withdrawals (a.k.a. transfers and replenishments), and can be linked together to create production steps.

HOW TO DO IT...

From the **Production flow** maintenance form, click on the **Activities** menu button within the **Versions** tab.

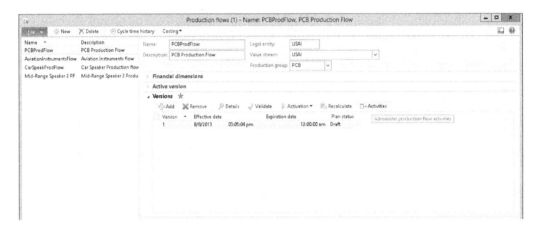

When the **Production flow activities** maintenance form is displayed, click on the **New version activity** button in the menu, and select the **Create new plan activity** option.

This will start the **Create new plan activity** wizard. Click on the **Next** button to start the process.

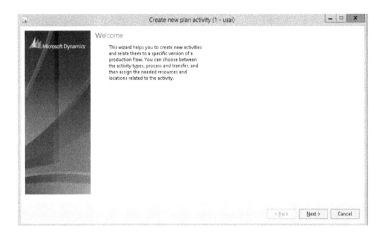

Select the **Activity type** from the dropdown options. To create a production activity,
use the *Process* option.

Leave all of the other defaults as they are and click the **Next** button to continue to the
next step.

In the next step, enter the **Resource group** that we created earlier on into the **Work cell**
field.

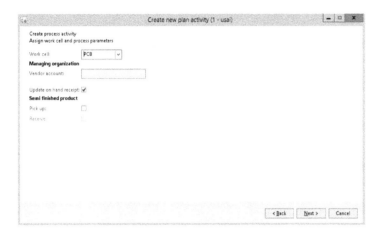

Then click **Next** to continue on.

In the next form, select the items that are going to be picked for the step in the Lean manufacturing assembly.

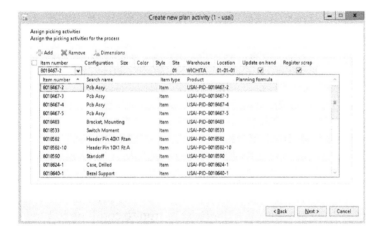

Then click the **Next** button to move to the next step.

Then define the default time and unit that it takes to perform the activity in the process.

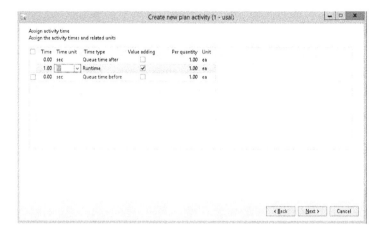

Once you have done that, click the **Next** button to continue on.

To finish the process, click on the **Finish** button on the wizard.

Now you will have an activity assigned to the **Production flow**.

Exit from the form by clicking on the **Close** button.

Activating Your Process Flow Version

The final step in the **Production flow** definition is to activate the version. Up until now we have not been able to do this because there were no activities assigned to the **Production Flow**.

HOW TO DO IT...

From the **Production flow** maintenance form, click on the **Activation** menu button within the **Versions** tab and select the **Activate** option.

When the **Activation** dialog box is displayed, click on the **OK** button to start the activation.

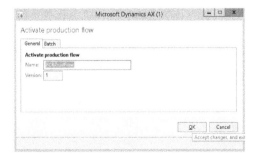

If everything has been set up correctly, then you will be able to activate your version, and then click on the **Close** button to exit the form.

Creating a Kanban Manufacturing Rule

The final piece that needs to be configured within the Lean Manufacturing process is a **Kanban Manufacturing Rule** which tells the system how to create your Kanban events that are associated with the your **Production Flows**. These events could be inventory movements, or production of product, and can be triggered by multiple scenarios within the Dynamics AX.

HOW TO DO IT...

From the **Production Control** area page, select the **Kanban rules** menu item from the **Lean manufacturing** folder within the **Setup** group.

When the **Kanban rules** maintenance form is displayed, click on the **Kanban rule** button within the **New** group of the **Setup** ribbon bar.

Select the type of Kanban event that you want to create from the **Type** dropdown. In this example we will select the *Manufacture* option.

Then from the **Replenishment strategy** field, select the type of way that you want to initiate the Kanban. In this example we will choose *Event* because we want this to be triggered from a Sales Order being placed.

If the **Multiple activities** check box is checked, uncheck it, because we don't want to chain activities together in this example.

From the **First plan activity** drop down, select the activity that we defined against the Production Flow in the earlier steps.

Within the **Details** tab, select the product that you want to manufacture as part of the Kanban Manufacturing step, and enter it into the **Product** field.

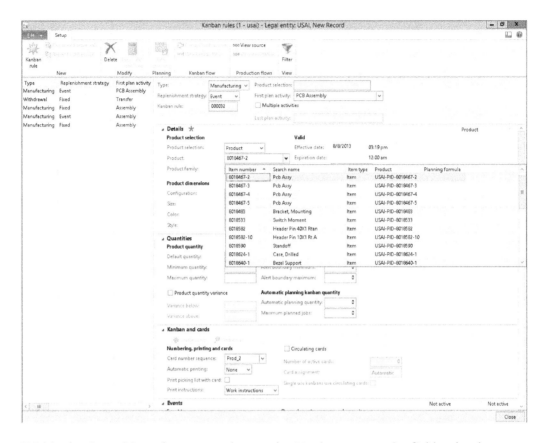

Within the **Quantities** tab, you can also set the **Maximum quantity** field to be the increment size for the planning and scheduling. I am setting this to 1 so that I can see every product that I need to plan at the each level. If you want to plan the production Kanbans at the order quantity level, then you can leave the value at 0.

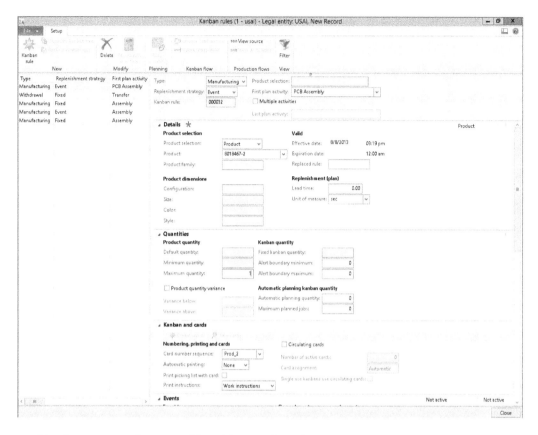

Within the **Events** tab, you will be able to select the **Sales event** type. This is the method that will trigger the Kanban. I selected *Automatic* in this example because I want the orders to show up on the Kanban planning board automatically when the orders are placed.

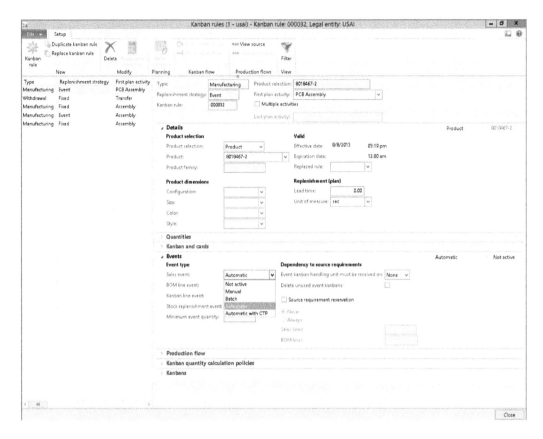

Once you have completed the setup, then you can click the **Close** button to exit out of the form.

Note: If you select the **Automatic** option for the Sales event, then it will give you a small warning, but you can ignore it.

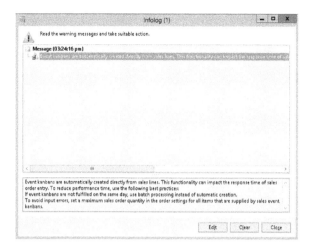

Now that we have defined our **Work Centers**, our **Production Flows,** and our **Kanban Rules** we can start placing orders and we will see the orders automatically being sent to our Kanban Scheduling board.

All we need to do in the system is create a Sales order for the product that we have defined the Kanban Sales Event for, and save the line.

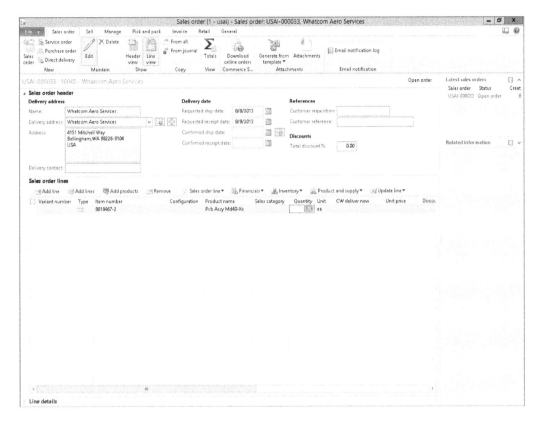

Then, from the **Production Control** area page, select the **Kanban Scheduling board** menu item from the **Lean manufacturing** folder within the **Common** group.

The lines from the order will automatically show up on the scheduling board, and will be waiting to be scheduled.

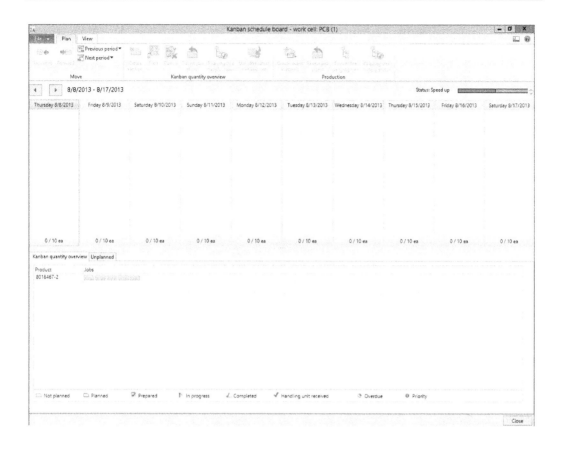

Assigning Tasks to Work Cells Through the Kanban Scheduling Board

Once the Kanbans are sent to the **Kanban Scheduling Board** they need to be then assigned to the work cells so that they will show up on their job reporting screen.

HOW TO DO IT...

To assign Kanbans to a Work Cell, just drag them from the Overview area at the bottom of the Kanban Schedule board up to the date that you want the Work Cell to perform the task.

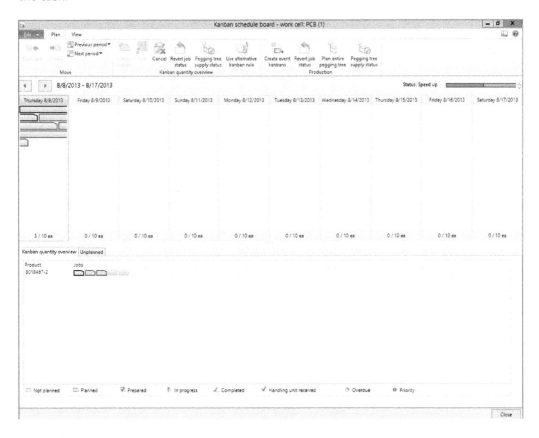

Reporting Jobs through the Kanban Board for Process Jobs

Once the Kanbans have been assigned to a **Work Cell** they will then be visible to the users through the **Kanban Board for Process Jobs** and they will be able to report the jobs started and completed through a single screen.

HOW TO DO IT...

From the **Production Control** area page, select the **Kanban board for process jobs** menu item from the **Lean manufacturing** folder within the **Common** group.

When the **Kanban board for process jobs** opens, you will see all of the production jobs that have been assigned to the work cell.

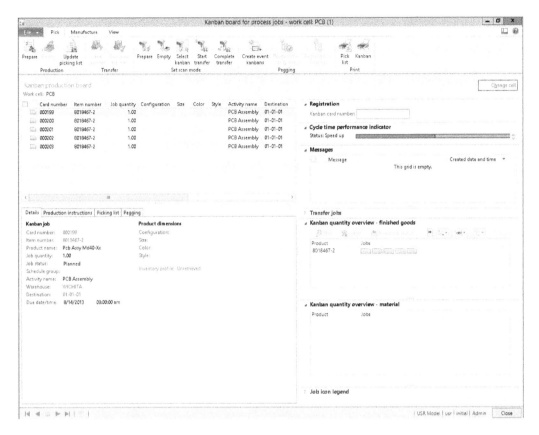

To start a job, just select the Kanban record, and click the **Start** button in the **Production** group of the **Manufacture** ribbon bar.

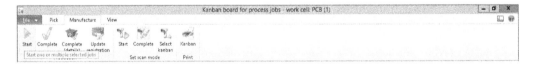

Once the job has been completed, click the **Complete** button in the **Production** group of the **Manufacture** ribbon bar.

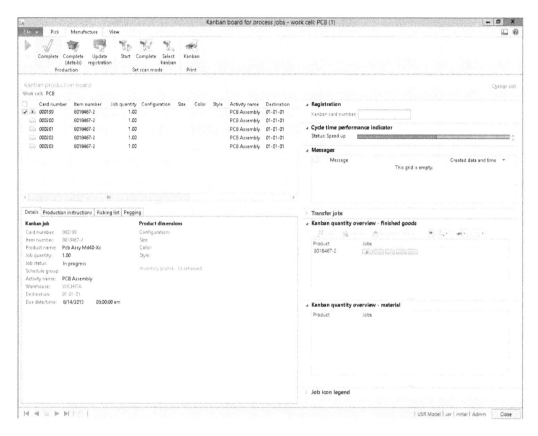

If we look at the inventory for the item, then we will see the inventory has been adjusted by the reporting of the item complete.

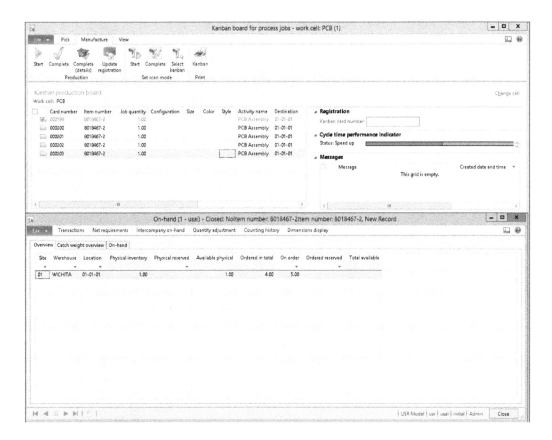

How cool is that.

Creating a Kanban Transfer Activity

Kanbans can also be related to inventory replenishment tasks. When inventory gets below a certain level, then Lean Manufacturing will automatically trigger replenishment of the Kanban bin.

HOW TO DO IT...

Open up the **Production Flow** that you just created, and in the **Versions** tab, click on the **Activites** button to open up the **Process Flow Activities** form.

Click on the **New version activity** menu item, and select the **Create new plan activity** option to create a new activity.

Step through the wizard, and when you get to the new activity page, select the *Transfer* option from the **Activity type** and then click the **Next** button.

On the next page, select the work cells that will be **Replenishing** and **Replenished** and click **Next**.

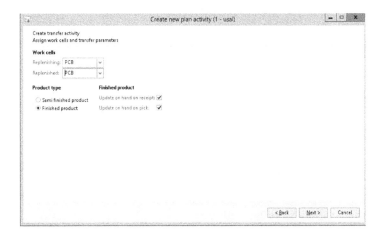

Then specify the To and from locations for the transfer, and click **Next**.

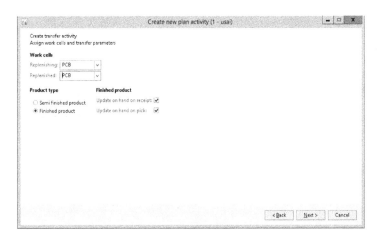

Then specify the To and from locations for the transfer, and click **Next**.

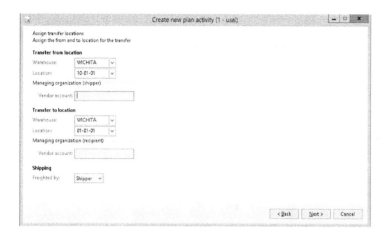

Finally specify the time for the transfer activity, and finish stepping through the wizard until it closes.

Once you have created the Transfer activity, click the **Close** button to exit the form.

Creating a Kanban Transfer Rule

The second step in configuring the Kanban Transfer is to create a rule that will tell the system how to replenish the location.

HOW TO DO IT...

From the **Production Control** area page, select the **Kanban rules** menu item from the **Lean manufacturing** folder within the **Setup** group.

When the **Kanban rules** maintenance form is displayed, click on the **Kanban rule** button within the **New** group of the **Setup** ribbon bar.

From the **Type** dropdown, select the **Withdrawal** option.

 This will allow you to select the Transfer replenishment activity that you defined in the last step.

Within the **Quantities** tab, set the **Default quantity** field to be the standard quantity that you want to start off with in the Kanban's (a.k.a. Bins) and then set the **Fixed kanban quantity** to be the number of Kanbans that you want to use.

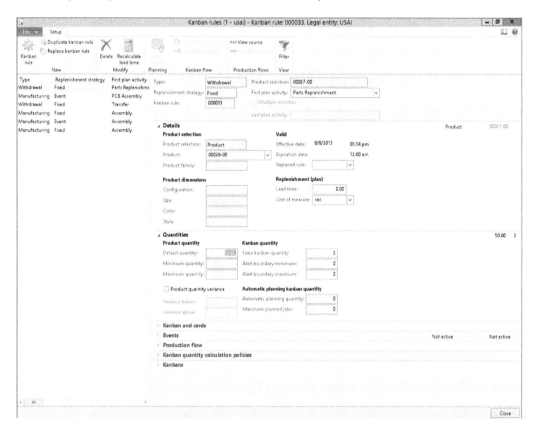

Since we are just creating this rule, we can tell the system to create the initial Kanbans by opening the **Kanbans** tab and then click on the **Add** menu button.

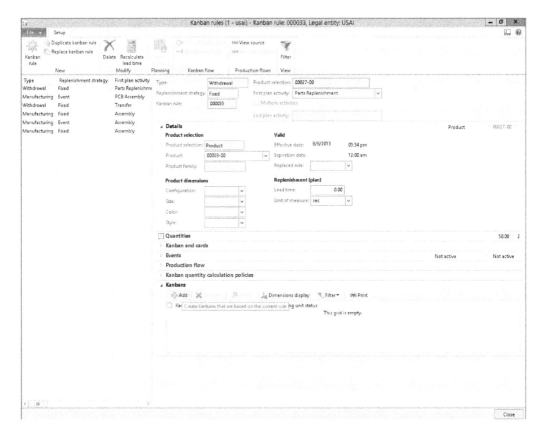

This will open up a dialog box that allows you to specify the number of Kanbans that you want to send initially to the Transfer Planning board.

Once you have done this, then you will see the Kanbans in the detail pane, and you can click on the **Close** button to exit the form.

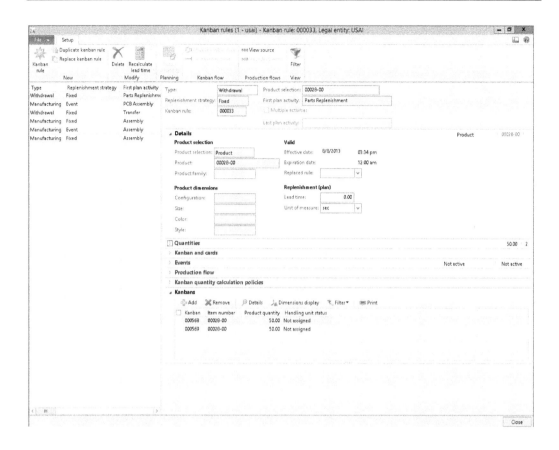

Executing Transfers through the Kanban Board for Transfer Jobs

Once the Withdrawal Kanbans are created within Dynamics AX, then they will show up for the inventory managers through the **Kanban Board for Transfer Jobs**, giving them a simple way to see what needs to go where within the warehouse.

HOW TO DO IT...

From the **Production Control** area page, select the **Kanban board for transfer jobs** menu item from the **Lean manufacturing** folder within the **Common** group.

Any transfers that have been suggested through Lean Manufacturing will automatically show up on this form.

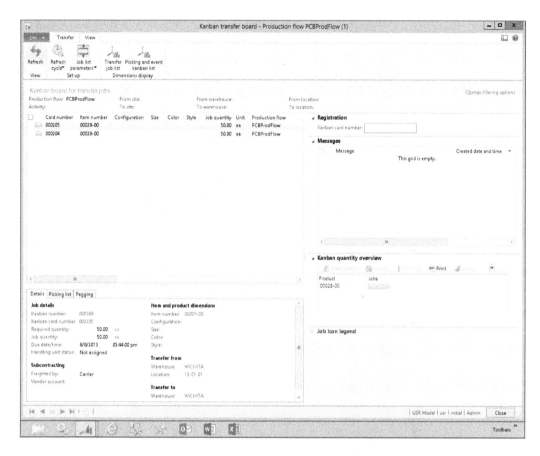

To start a picking process, click on the Kanban withdrawal that you want to start the transfer on, and click the **Start** button within the **Transfer** group of the **Transfer** ribbon bar.

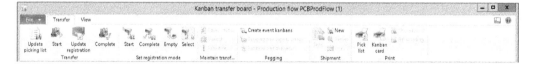

If you look at the inventory, then the from warehouse location will show the commitment for the transfer, and the to location will show the expected quantity that is about to be received.

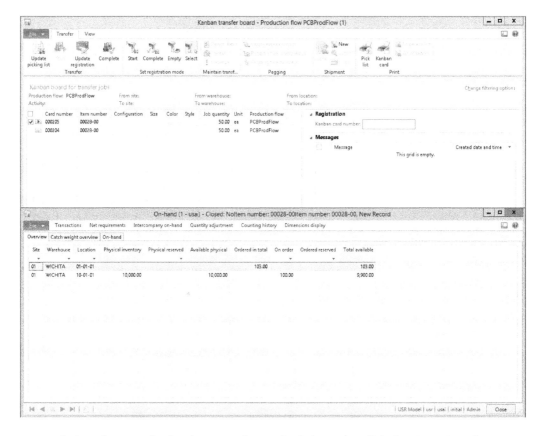

To mark that the transfer has been performed, click on the click the **Complete** button within the **Transfer** group of the **Transfer** ribbon bar.

Looking at the inventory levels will show that the inventory has been transferred.

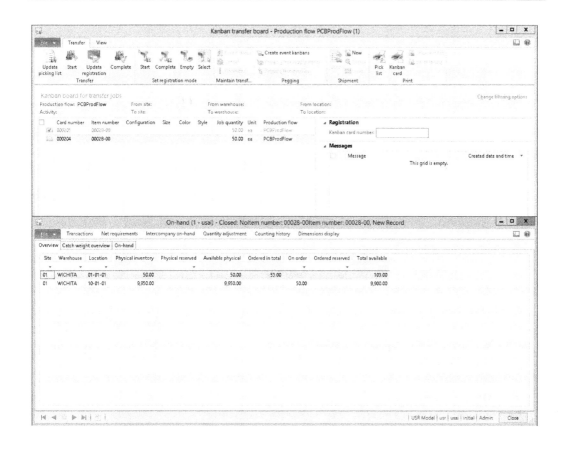

Marking Transfer Kanbans as Empty through the Transfer Board

The **Kanban Board for Transfer Jobs** has an additional function that we will highlight which allows the user to mark Kanbans as being empty. When this is done, then the replenishment Kanbans for the work cell will be automatically created.

HOW IT WORKS...

From the **Kanban Board for Transfer Jobs**, you can select the Kanban that is currently empty on the right hand side, within the **Kanban quantity overview** panel, and then click the **Empty** menu button to mark the Kanban as empty.

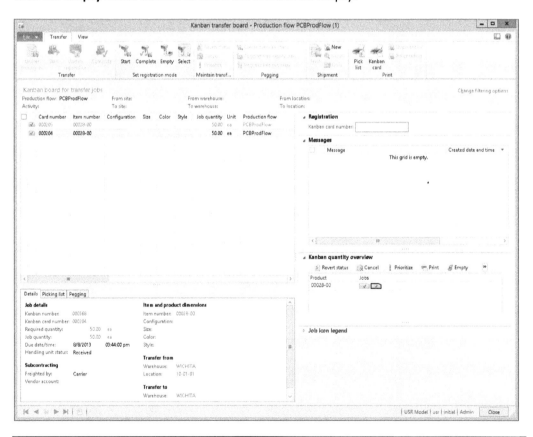

The Transfer Board will make a note in the **Messages** tab that the Kanban was emptied.

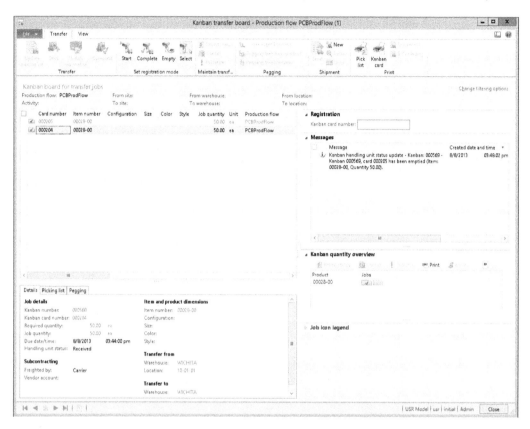

And the next time that the Kanban view is refreshed, a new replenishment order will appear.

How cool is that!

Summary

In this worked example we worked through the setup of a set of simple production and transfer Kanbans. The interesting thing about these processes, is that you don't necessarily need to be a Lean Manufacturer in order to take advantage of these capabilities. For piece work, then this process works really well, and also the transfer Kanbans can easily be used by traditional manufacturers to replenish floor stocking areas.

Once you have worked through these examples, you may want to branch out and try other areas of the Lean Manufacturing that we didn't address in this presentation. Features that you may want to try include:

- Having multiple activities in a Process Flow that are chained together.

- Using the bar code scanning to further automate the job reporting process

- Using the planning and scheduling in conjunction with the Lean Manufacturing to create the purchase forecasts etc.

This is a really useful feature within Dynamics AX. Just because you have always used BOM's and Routes does not mean that you can't dabble in Process Flows and Activities. Give it a try and I'm sure you will like what you find out.

Configuring Service Management to track Service Orders

The Service Management area within Dynamics AX allows you to track all of your service order contracts and service orders for your customers, will track all of your time and expenses against the service orders, and will also pass along any chargeable items to the receivables department for automatic invoicing to the customer.

Service Management has additional functions as well that allow you to track the items that are being serviced, define the tasks that are allowed to be performed against a service order, and also track the symptoms, diagnosis, and resolution to service order issues, making it a great tracking and analysis tool.

In this walkthrough we will show how you can create service agreements and orders, and then how you can use the additional tracking features within Service Management to get a tighter handle on your service orders.

Creating a Service Agreement

Service Agreements are the basis for all of your service orders. They allow you to define the default structures of your **Service Orders** and also link back to the project management area so that you are able to bill for any activity that has been performed against the service orders. As a result, the first step in the process of configuring **Service Management** is to create a **Service Agreement.**

HOW TO DO IT...

From the **Service Management** area page, select the **Service agreements** menu item from within the **Service agreements** folder of the **Common** group.

When the **Service Agreements** list page opens up, click on the **Agreement wizard** button within the **New** group of the **Service agreement** ribbon bar.

When the **Service Agreement** wizard is displayed, click then **Next** button to start the process.

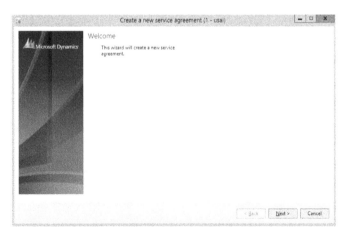

Select the **Customer account** that you would like the service agreement to be associated with.

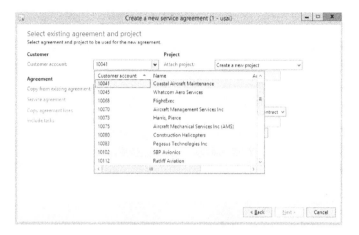

Then select the *Create a new project* option from the **Attach project** drop down to tell the system that we want to create an entirely new project to track this information.

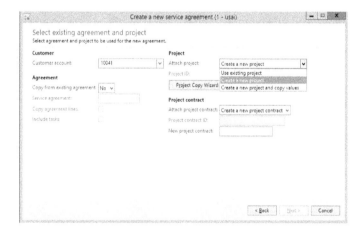

Note: If you have already created a project for the customer, and would like to mingle the Service Agreements, then you can select the *Use existing project* option.

Within the **Project contract** group, enter a description of the Service Agreement into the **New project contract** field.

When you have done this, click on the **Next** button to move to the next step in the wizard.

For the new project creation defaults, select *Time and material* for the **Project Type**.

Select a **Project group**.

Enter the name of the Service Agreement into the **Project name** field so that we can easily trace the project back to the agreement.

Finally set the default **Line property**. In this case we want all lines to be chargeable unless we override the value.

When the project defaults have been defined click on the **Next** button to continue to the next step.

For the new agreement creation defaults, enter a **Description** for the Service Agreement.

Enter a date into the **Start date** field to specify when you want the agreement to be effective.

If you want to have default service technicians to be associated with this **Service Agreement** then you can also specify those here as well.

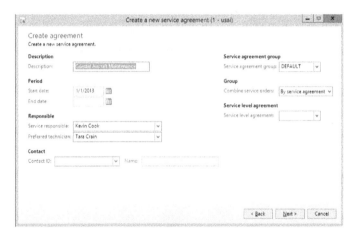

When you have configures the defaults for the **Service Agreement** click the **Next** button to continue on.

When you reach the confirmation page, click the **Finish** button to have the system create your **Service Agreement**.

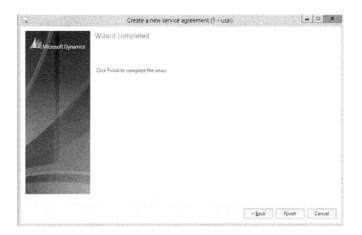

You should receive an Infolog box showing that the **Service Agreement** has been created.

Creating a Service Order

Once you have a **Service Agreement** you can start creating **Service Orders** and posting time and material against them.

HOW TO DO IT...

From the **Service Management** area page, select the **Service orders** menu item from within the **Service orders** folder of the **Common** group.

When the **Service Orders** list page opens up, click on the **Service order** button within the **New** group of the **Service order** ribbon bar.

Enter a description of the **Service Order** into the **Description** field.

Within the **Reference** group select your **Service Agreement** that you set up in the previous step.

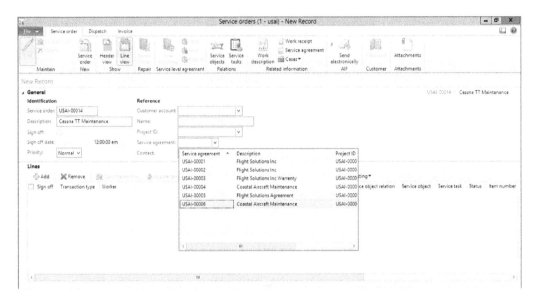

This will default in the **Customer account**, and the **Project ID** for you.

Alternatively, you can select the **Customer account** from the dropdown, and then select the **Service agreement** from the filtered list.

Posting Time to a Service Order

Once you have a **Service Order** record, you can start posting time and materials to it, and recording activity.

HOW TO DO IT...

From within the **Lines** tab on the **Service order** click on the **Add** button in the tool bar to create a new service order line.

To post time against the **Service Order** select *Hour* from the **Transaction type** drop down.

Select the **Category** for the line from the drop down to specify the type of labor that is being assigned to the **Service Order**.

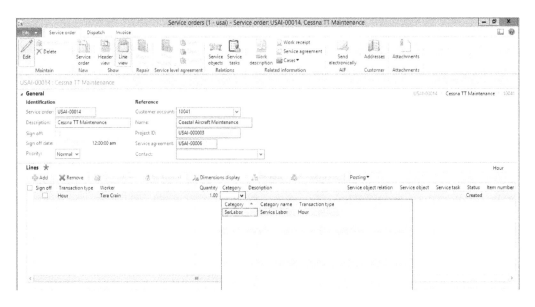

Note: If you drill into the **Project Categories** then make sure that the **Active in journals** check box is marked.

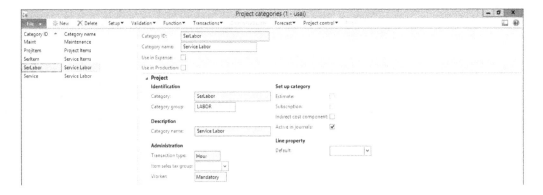

Also, if you want to update the default costs and prices for the labor that is being assigned to the **Service Order** then select wither the **Cost price** or **Sales price** options from the **Setup** menu item.

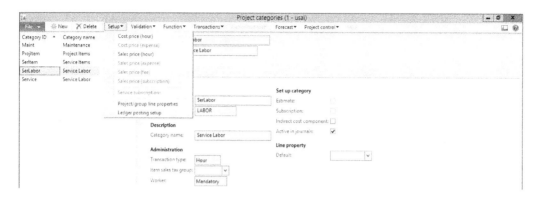

This will allow you to specify the default rates that will be applied when these **Project categories** are used on a **Service Order**.

Posting through the Service Management Portal

The Service Management area also has a web portal that allows you to view and update **Service Orders**, and **Agreements** through a web site.

HOW IT WORKS...

The **Service management portal** is part of the default Enterprise Portal. As soon as you access it, you will be able to see all of the same information that is available through the traditional windows client.

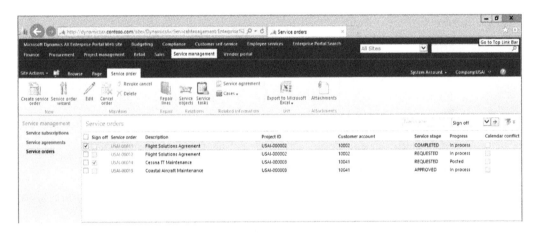

You are able to add service lines through the web site as well.

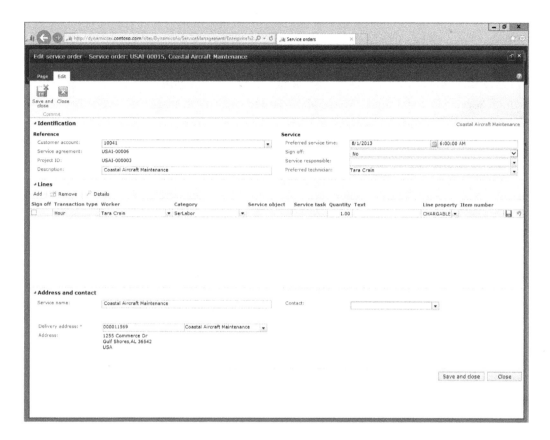

How cool is that.

Configuring Service Order Stages

If you want to track the lifecycle of your **Service Orders** then you can easily do this through **Service Order Stages**. These allow you to define the stages that your Service Order will progress through, what transactions can be performed at any of the stages, and also when the Service Order is closed or not.

HOW TO DO IT...

From the **Service management** area page, select the **Service stages** menu item from within the **Service orders** folder of the **Setup** group.

When the **Service stages** maintenance form is displayed, click on the **New** button in the menu bar to create the initial stage.

Give your stage a **Service stage** code, and a **Description**.

Then mark the valid operations that can be performed at the stage.

Note: You can use the **Service Stages** to manage when lines can be posted, if deletions are allowed and a lot more.

Continue adding additional stages to your **Service stages**, but for each additional stage, you will need to specify the parent **Service stage.**

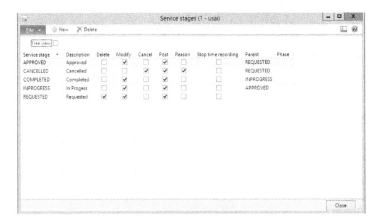

Note: If you check the **Tree view** check box, then you will be able to see the complete route for the stages.

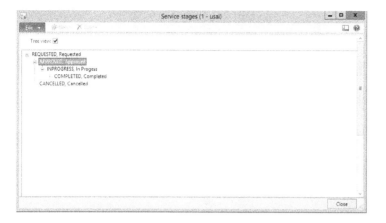

To change the state of the **Service Order**, just select the record, and then click on the **Next Stage** button within the **Service stage** group of the **Dispatch** ribbon bar.

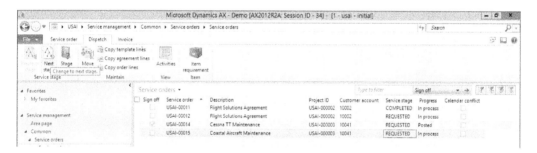

If you have defined multiple options for the next stage in the process, then you will be asked which stage you would like to move the **Service Order** into. Select the option, and then click the **OK** button.

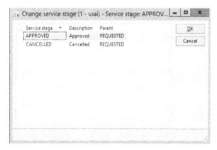

Now you will see that the **Service stage** for the **Service Order** has change the next stage in the process.

Configuring Service Reason Codes

If you mark any of the **Service Order Stages** to as having a **Reason** then you will also need to add a set of reason codes Dynamics AX for the **Service Stages** to reference.

HOW TO DO IT...

From the **Service management** area page, select the **Service reason codes** menu item from within the **Service orders** folder of the **Setup** group.

When the **Service reason code** maintenance form is displayed, click on the **New** button in the menu bar to create the initial stage.

Give your stage a **Service reason code**, and a **Description**.

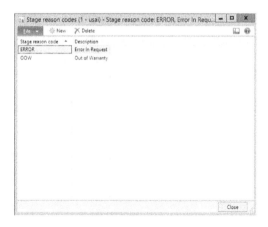

Continue adding additional reason codes, and when you are finished, click on the **Close** button to exit the form.

Signing Off and Posting Service Order Lines

Once you have entered time and materials against a **Service Order** you can approve the lines by signing off on them, and also post the lines to the project allowing them to be tracked and also invoiced.

HOW TO DO IT...

Select any of the lines that you want to approve for posting, and expand the **Line details** tab so that you can see the **General** subtab.

To approve the line, just check the **Sign off** check box.

Once the line has been approved, you will be able to select the **Post service order line** option from the **Postings** drop down menu within the **Lines** group.

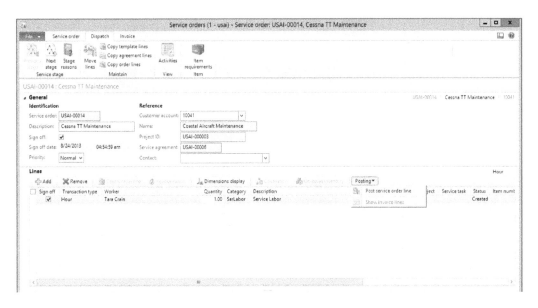

When the **Post service orders** dialog box is displayed, select a to and from date that you want to capture the time and materials from, and also check the transactions that you want to include in the postings.

When you are ready to post the lines, click on the **OK** button.

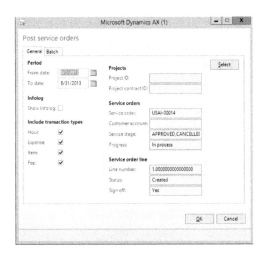

If there are unposted transactions, then you will receive an Infolog that tells you that they have been posted to a journal.

Once your transactions have been posted, you can view them against the projects that are associated with the **Service Agreement**.

From the **Project management and accounting** area page, select the **All projects** menu item from within the **Projects** folder of the **Common** group.

Select the project that is associated with your **Service Agreement**.

From the **Manage** ribbon bar, click on the **Posted transactions** menu item within the **Related information** group.

This will show you all of the transactions that have been transferred from the **Service Order** over to the **Project.**

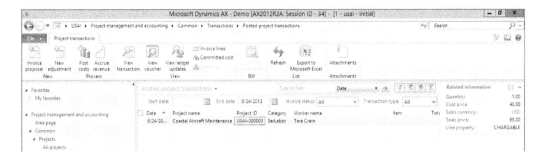

Drilling into the record will show you more information about the line item.

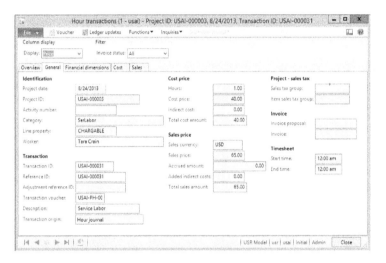

Invoicing Service Orders Time & Material

Once you have posted the transactions to your **Service Agreement Project** you can use the **Invoice Proposal** function to automatically generate the invoice transactions for the customer so that they can be processed by the receivables department.

HOW TO DO IT...

From the Project management and accounting area page, select the Posted project transactions menu item from within the Transactions folder of the Common group.

This will show you a list of all the transactions posted through the Projects.

From the New group of the Project transactions ribbon bar, click on the Invoice proposal button.

When the Create invoice proposal dialog appears, it will show all of the uninvoiced transactions. To create the invoice proposals, just click on the OK button.

You will now be taken to the Invoice proposal that was created from the transactions. To convert the Invoice proposal into an AR Invoice click on the Post button within the Functions group of the Invoice proposal ribbon bar.

If you want to Print the Invoice, then you can check the option on the Posting dialog box. When you are ready to post, click the OK button.

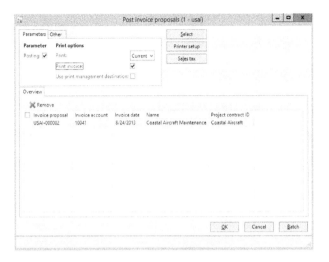

The Invoice Posting process will show you the invoice that is generated. You can automatically email this to your customer as well through the print management function.

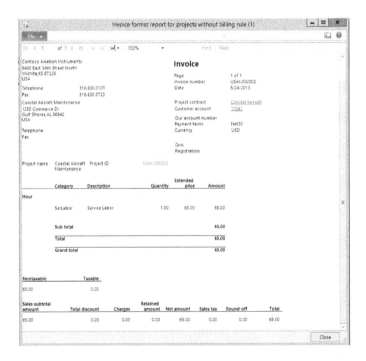

If you look within the Receivables area, you will also see the invoice transaction has now been added to the customer account.

Creating Project Statements for Service Agreements

As you start accruing time and expenses against your **Service Agreement** you can take advantage of the **Project Statements** function within the **Projects** to track how much the agreement is costing, and if you are breaking even.

HOW IT WORKS...

From the **Project management and accounting** area page, select the **All projects** menu item from within the **Projects** folder of the **Common** group.

Click on the **Project Statements** button within the **Statements** group of the **Control** ribbon bar.

The first time that the **Project Statements** dialog box is displayed for a project, it will not show any information. To populate the statement, specify the from and to dates for the statement and then click on the **Calculate** option in the menu bar.

The system will now show you a break down on all of the costs and revenue for the project.

You can also create a pivot table view of this data within Excel by clicking on the **Export to Microsoft Excel** button in the menu bar.

When the Export dialog box is displayed, specify a file location for the statement, select the dimensions that you want to export to Excel, and then click on the **OK** button.

This will create a Statement for your project within Excel.

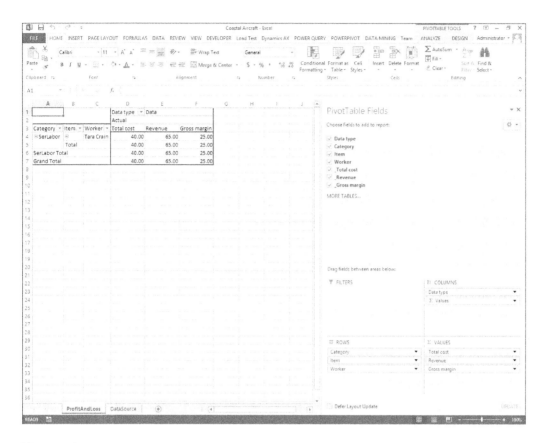

Very cool.

Creating Periodic Service Intervals

If you have service orders that repeat on a regular basis, then you can configure **Service Intervals** and then assign them to lines on your **Service Agreements** and then have the **Service Management** area automatically generate the Service Order jobs for you.

HOW TO DO IT...

From the **Service management** area page, select the **Service intervals** menu item from within the **Service agreements** folder of the **Setup** group.

When the **Service intervals** dialog box is displayed, you can create new intervals by clicking on the **New** button in the menu bar.

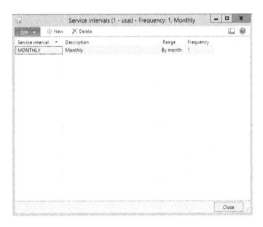

Give your **Service Interval** a code and description, and from the **Range** dropdown, select the general time frame that you want to manage the interval in.

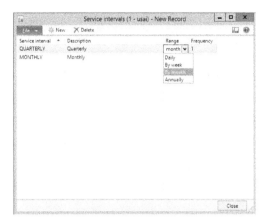

Then within the **Frequency** field select the number of Ranges that you want to space the interval.

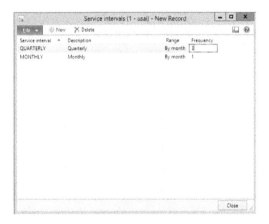

Repeat the process for all of the different intervals that you can think of.

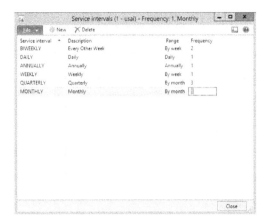

To use the **Service Interval** open up your **Service Agreement** and add a new line. Within the **Service Interval** field, select the frequency that you want to perform the service order task.

And then specify the start date for the task so that the frequency has a beginning.

Creating Periodic Service Orders

From the **Service management** area page, select the **Create service orders** menu item from within the **Service orders** folder of the **Periodic** group.

HOW TO DO IT...

From the **Service management** area page, select the **Create service orders** menu item from within the **Service orders** folder of the **Periodic** group.

When the service order creation dialog box appears, select a to and from date that you want to search for recurring service order tasks, and also select the transaction types that you want to include. Then click the **OK** button.

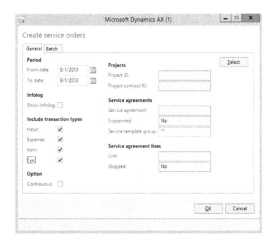

If there are **Service Agreement** lines that fall within your date range and transaction type, the system will notify you that they have been created.

You will see the new **Service Orders** automatically show up.

Drilling into the detail you will be able to see the task that was assigned to the work order.

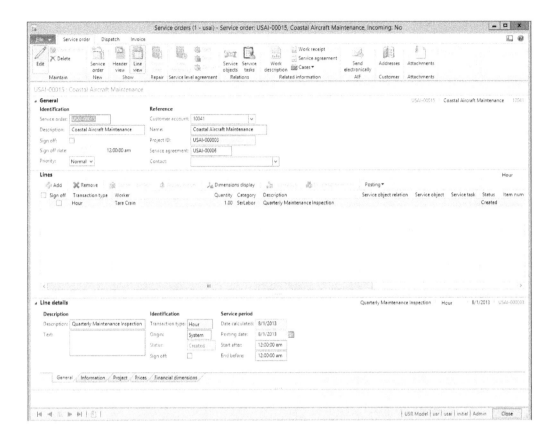

Printing Service Orders

Once the **Service Orders** are created, you can also print them.

HOW IT WORKS...

From your **Service Order** click on the **Work Description** button within the **Related Information** group of the **Service Orders** ribbon bar.

When the print dialog is displayed, select the options that you want to include in the **Work Instructions** and then click the **OK** button.

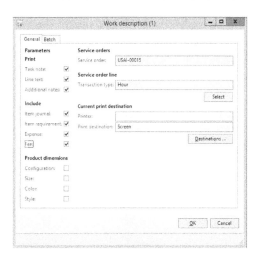

This will print out all of your work instructions for you technician to use and sign off on.

Creating Service Objects

The **Service Management** area allows you to track what the **Service Orders** and **Service Agreements** are related to through what a called **Service Objects**. A Service Object could be something that is tracked as in inventoried item, or it could just be a reference to something that is being serviced.

HOW TO DO IT...

From the **Service management** area page, select the **Service objects** menu item from within the **Service objects** folder of the **Setup** group.

When the **Service objects** maintenance form is displayed, click on the **New** button in the menu bar to create a new record.

All you need to specify for the **Service Object** is the **Description** and the **Service object group**.

When you have defined all of your **Service Objects** click on the **Close** button to exit the form.

Assigning Service Objects to Service Agreements

Once you have defined your **Service Objects** you can start assigning them to your **Service Agreements** and **Service Orders**.

HOW TO DO IT...

The first step is to associate a **Service Object** with your **Service Agreement**. To do this, open up your **Service Agreement** and then click on the **Service object** button within the **Relations** group of the **Service Agreement** ribbon bar.

Then the **Service objects** maintenance form is displayed, click on the **New** button in the menu bar.

From the **Service Object** dropdown box, select the **Service Object** that you configured in the previous step.

You can continue adding **Service Objects** to the **Service Agreement**.

When you are done, click on the **Close** button to exit the form.

Now you will be able to associate the **Service Object** with any of the lines on your **Service Agreement** and get better reporting.

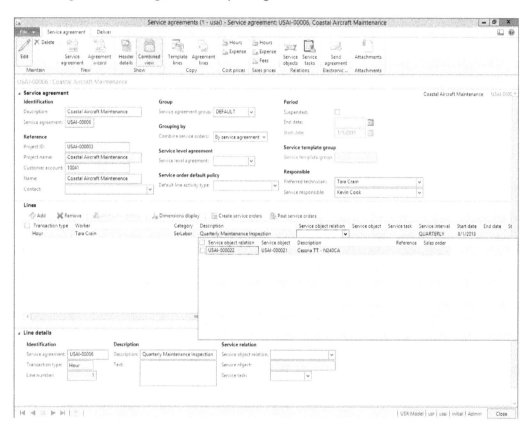

Creating Service Tasks

You can also define the tasks that you are allowed to perform against a **Service Agreement** as well through the **Service Tasks**.

HOW TO DO IT...

From the **Service management** area page, select the **Service tasks** menu item from the **Setup** group.

Within the **Service tasks** maintenance form, click the **New** button in the menu bar to create a **Service task** record.

Then assign your **Service task** a code and **Description**.

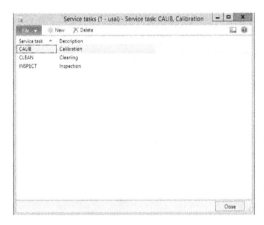

Repeat this process to add as many **Service Tasks** as you like and then click the **Close** button to exit the form.

Assigning Valid Service Tasks to Agreements

Once you have defined your **Service Tasks** you can start assigning them to your **Service Agreement** and **Service Order** lines.

HOW TO DO IT...

The first step is to associate a **Service Task** with your **Service Agreement**. To do this, open up your **Service Agreement** and then click on the **Service tasks** button within the **Relations** group of the **Service Agreement** ribbon bar.

Then the **Service tasks** maintenance form is displayed, click on the **New** button in the menu bar.

From the **Service task** dropdown box, select the **Service tasks** that you configured in the previous step.

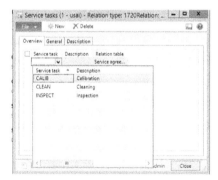

If you switch to the **Description** tab, you can also include internal and external comments and notes for the tasks.

You can continue adding **Service tasks** to the **Service Agreement**.

When you are done, click on the **Close** button to exit the form.

Now you will be able to associate the **Service task** with any of the lines on your **Service Agreement** and get better reporting.

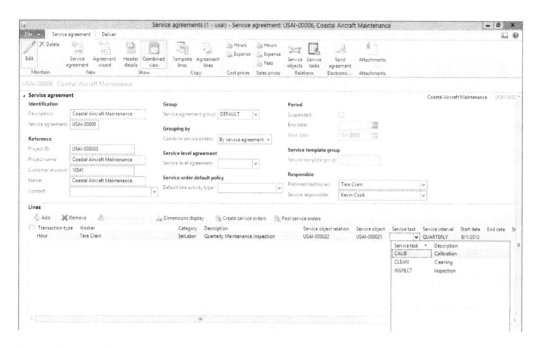

Note: If you add multiple lines to your **Service Agreement** then you can start differentiating the tasks that are being performed.

Defining Repair Conditions

The **Service Management** area also allows you to track repairs that have been performed as part of the **Service Order** process. The first part of this process allows you to define a set of **Repair Conditions** which are general repair categories.

HOW TO DO IT...

From the **Service management** area page, select the **Conditions** menu item from the **Repair** folder of the **Setup** group.

When the **Conditions** maintenance for is displayed, click on the **New** button in the menu bar to create a new **Condition** record.

Then add a **Condition** code and a **Description** for the condition.

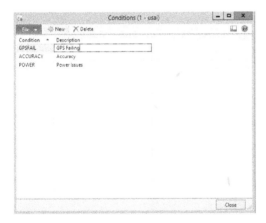

Continue adding **Conditions** and when you have finished, click on the **Close** button to exit the form.

This will open up the **Ratings** maintenance form with all of the **Evaluation Criteria Groups** listed on the left, and all of the **Evaluation Criteria** for that group on the right.

Defining Repair Symptoms & Codes

The next piece of information that you can track on repairs are the **Repair Symptoms**. These are usually the initial symptoms that are reported that initiate the **Service Order**. They may not be the actual cause of the problem, but they may be the most noticeable ones. There can also be two levels to the **Symptoms**, the **Area** which would be where the problem was reported, and also an optional sub-symptom called the **Symptom code** which may describe what was happening to the **Symptom Area.**

HOW TO DO IT...

From the **Service management** area page, select the **Symptom areas** menu item from the **Repair** folder of the **Setup** group.

When the **Symptom area** maintenance for is displayed, click on the **New** button in the menu bar to create a new **Symptom area** record.

Then add a **Symptom area** code and a **Description** for the condition.

Continue adding **Symptom areas** until you have created them all.

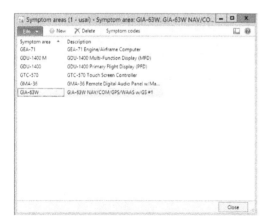

If you want to add more detail to the **Symptom areas** then you can click on the **Symptom codes** menu item to open up the **Symptom codes** maintenance form.

To add a sub-category of the **Symptom code**, click on the **New** button in the menu bar to create a new **Symptom code** record and then add a **Symptom code** and a **Description**.

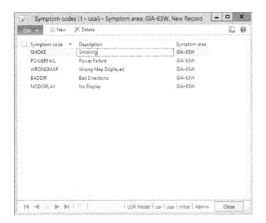

Continue adding you **Symptom codes** and when you have finished, click on the **Close** button to exit the form.

Defining Repair Diagnosis Areas

The **Service Management** area also allows you to track the **Repair Diagnosis** on the **Repair**. These are usually the actual problems diagnosed by the technician during the **Service Order**. There can be two levels to the **Diagnosis**, the **Area** which would be what the problem is, and also an optional **Diagnosis code** which describes how to fix the problem.

HOW TO DO IT...

From the **Service management** area page, select the **Diagnosis areas** menu item from the **Repair** folder of the **Setup** group.

When the **Diagnosis area** maintenance for is displayed, click on the **New** button in the menu bar to create a new **Diagnosis area** record.

Then add a **Diagnosis area** code and a **Description**.

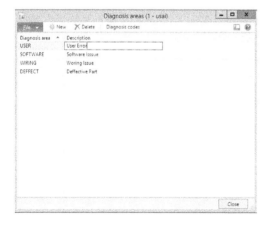

Continue adding **Diagnosis areas** until you have created them all.

If you want to add more detail to the **Diagnosis areas** then you can click on the **Diagnosis codes** menu item to open up the **Diagnosis codes** maintenance form.

To add a sub-category of the **Diagnosis code**, click on the **New** button in the menu bar to create a new **Diagnosis code** record and then add a **Diagnosis code** and a **Description**.

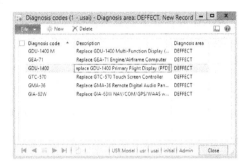

Continue adding you **Diagnosis codes** and when you have finished, click on the **Close** button to exit the form.

Defining Repair Resolutions

The final piece of information that you can configure to track the repairs is the **Repair Resolution**. This is used to track what was done to complete the repair, and you can use it for reporting and analysis.

HOW TO DO IT...

From the **Service management** area page, select the **Resolutions** menu item from the **Repair** folder of the **Setup** group.

When the **Resolutions** maintenance for is displayed, click on the **New** button in the menu bar to create a new **Resolution** record.

Then add a **Resolution** code and a **Description** for the condition.

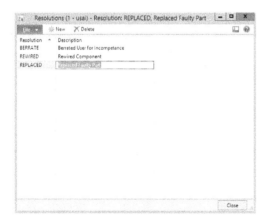

Continue adding **Resolutions** and when you have finished, click on the **Close** button to exit the form.

Defining Repair Stages

If you want to, you also have the option to track the **Repair Stages**, so that you can track the progress of repairs.

HOW TO DO IT...

From the **Service management** area page, select the **Repair stage** menu item from the **Repair** folder of the **Setup** group.

When the **Repair stages** maintenance for is displayed, click on the **New** button in the menu bar to create a new **Repair stage** record.

Then add a **Repair stage** code, a **Description** for the condition, and if the stage is the end of the process, then check the **Finished** check box.

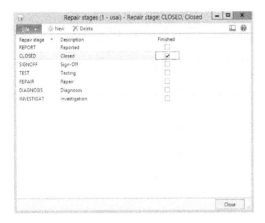

Continue adding **Repair stages** and when you have finished, click on the **Close** button to exit the form.

This will open up the **Ratings** maintenance form with all of the **Evaluation Criteria Groups** listed on the left, and all of the **Evaluation Criteria** for that group on the right.

Recording Repair Operations

Once all of the codes have been configured for your **Repair** process, you can now start tracking the repairs against **Service Orders** and **Agreements**. This is a great way to track what has been done in the past, and also if a **Service Order** is being continually raised against a **Service Agreement** or a **Service Object** then you can start tracking if the resolutions for the repairs are actually working.

HOW IT WORKS...

To start the **Repair** tracking process, select your **Service Order** that you are working on, and then click the **Repair lines** button within the **Repair** group of the **Service Orders** ribbon bar.

When the **Repair Lines** maintenance form is displayed, click the **New** button in the menu bar to create a new **Repair** record.

Select the **Condition** (the general problem) from the drop down list.

If you know the area that the problem is being reported to happen then you can select it form the **Symptom area** drop down box.

If you have additional details about the **Symptom**, then you can also select it from the **Symptom code** drop down list.

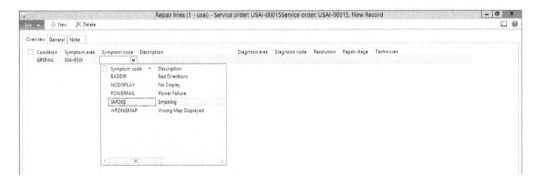

In the **Description** field, enter in a brief description of the problem.

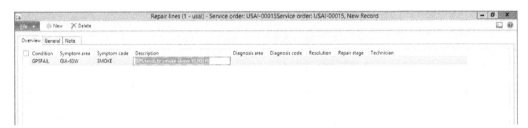

If you have a more detailed description, then select the **Note** tab, and you will be able to enter a virtually unlimited number of lines in the **Text** field.

As more information is gathered on the **Repair** then you can also update the **Diagnosis area**, the **Diagnosis code**, and the **Resolution.**

When you have finished updating the **Repair** click the **Close** button to exit out of the form.

Summary

In this walkthrough we have shown a number of the features that you can easily take advantage of within the **Service Management** area of Dynamics AX. By leveraging the **Project accounting** area, the **Service Management** functions give you a lot of power without having to invest a lot of effort in the setup.

You can use many of these features to track both external and internal service projects, so you may want to try using this for:

- Customer Service Orders (as we have shown in this example)
- Simple internal maintenance repair operations
- Help desk support tracking

Additionally, there are features that we did not describe in the walk through that you may want to investigate. They include:

- Using the dispatch board to schedule technicians
- Sourcing repair items from inventory
- Creation of Service Orders from projects

Take a look at the **Service Management** module, it's simple to configure, and could help a lot.

Configuring and Using Vendor Requests

Built into Dynamics AX is a feature for managing the setup of new Vendors which allows users to request for new vendors to be added, for the purchasing group approval process by the way of workflows, and finally automatically create new vendor records. Additionally, if you are using the Vendor Portal, the on-boarding process will allow you to co-ordinate the setup of the vendor users, and if you want to, you van also have the prospective vendors update and approve their information before they are approved to ensure that their details are correct, and that they want to do business with you as well. This process is a great way to streamline the vendor setup process and is also a time saver because people are involved through the workflow process and all activities are tracked.

In this blueprint we will show how the vendor on-boarding process is handled through the Vendor Requests function within Dynamics AX.

Configuring the Vendor Justification Workflow

Before we start the first step in the process we need to create a simple workflow for the approval of the initial new vendor request. This will allow the purchasing department to quickly weed out the requests that shouldn't be considered in the first place.

HOW TO DO IT...

From the **Setup** group on the **Procurement and sourcing** area page, click on the **Procurement and sourcing workflows** menu item.

If you do not already have a **Vendor add justification workflow** defined, click on the **New** button in the **New** group of the **Workflow** ribbon bar.

When the procurement workflow template selection dialog box is displayed, select the **Vendor add justification workflow** template and click the **Create workflow** button to create the workflow shell.

When you return to the **Procurement and sourcing workflows** form, double-click on the

Vendor add justification workflow workflow to open up the designer.

When the workflow designer is displayed, create a simple flow that just has the **Approve new vendor justification** step and then click on the **Save and close** button to save and activate the workflow.

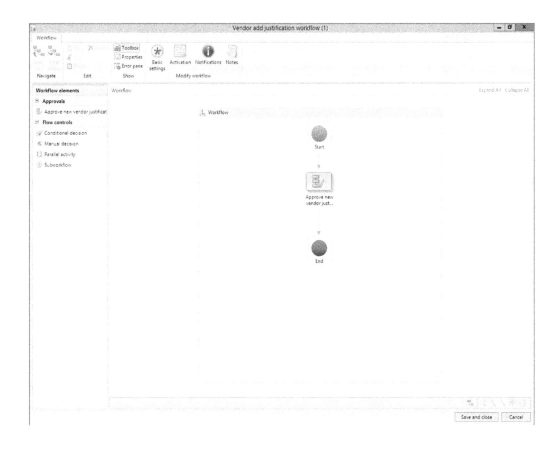

Creating a New Vendor Request via the Employee Self Service Portal

Once you have the **Vendor add justification workflow** defined, users are able to request new vendors through the Employee Self Service Portal and then submit them for approval.

HOW TO DO IT...

New Vendor Requests are initiated from the **Employee Self Service Portal** by clicking on the **Vendor requests** link within the **Order Products** group.

When the **Vendor requests** form is displayed, click on the **Vendor request** button within the **New** group of the **Requests** ribbon bar.

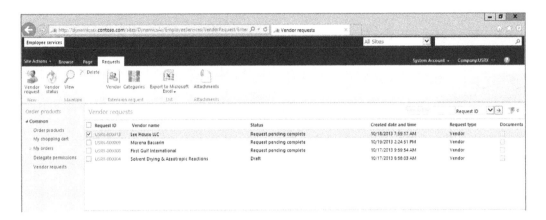

When the **New vendor request** dialog box is displayed, fill in the **Vendor Name**, and also the **First name** and **Last name** of the main contact that you have for the new vendor.

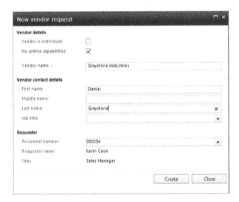

Note: In this example we also checked the **No online capabilities** box to simplify the process. At the end of this walkthrough we will show what additional steps are enabled when this checkbox remains unchecked.

After you have filled in the basic information, click on the **Create** button to create your new vendor request.

This will now take you to a more detailed form where you can start filling out more information about the vendor. Start off by opening up the **Vendor address details** tab, and clicking on the **Add** button to add a new address for the requested vendor.

Update the address details for the vendor request and then click on the **Save and close** button to return to the maintenance form.

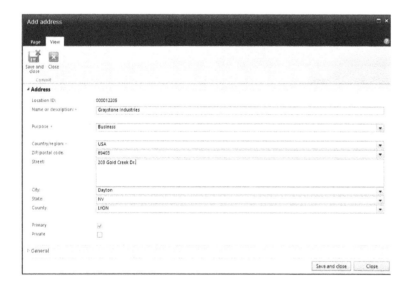

Then open up the **Vendor contact details** and add any relevant contact information like e-mails and phone numbers.

If you have personal contact information for the contact person, then open up the **Contact person contact details** tab, click on the **Add** button and add that information as well.

We need to add at least one entry in the **Procurement details** category list.

And finally open up the **Business justification** tab and fill in any of the information that the Purchasing department have configured as a justification checklist.

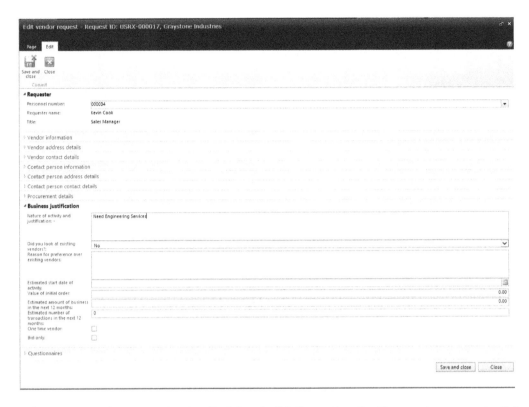

When you are done entering in all of the shell information for the vendor request, click on the **Save and close** button to update the information.

Once you have saved the data, then you will be able to see a **Submit** button in the workflow toolbar. To start the approval process, just click the **Submit** button.

If you have any comments that you want to attach to the submission then you can add them in the **Comments** dialog box, and then click the **Submit** button.

Now you will be able to see your new vendor request, and also see the status of the request which should be **Request submitted.**

Approving New Vendor Add Justification Requests

Once the new vendor request has been submitted, the workflow that you configured for the **Vendor add justification** will start notifying the necessary people that there are requests that need to be approved.

HOW TO DO IT...

Once a new vendor request has been submitted, if the user is involved in the approval process then they will receive notifications through all of the channels that you have associated with the workflow, including the notification list and also the pop-up notifications through the tool bar.

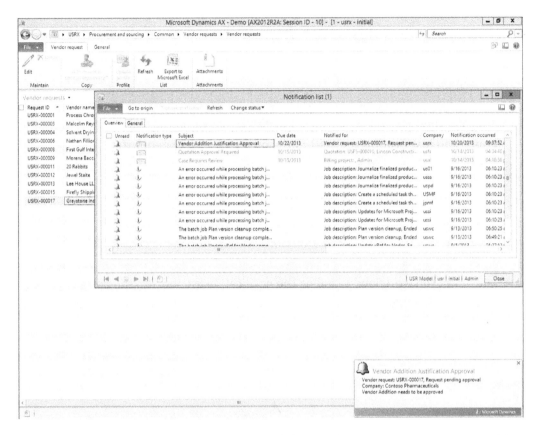

To sell all of the new vendor requests, click on the **Vendor Requests** menu item within the **Vendor requests** folder of the **Common** group of the **Procurement and sourcing** area page.

As new vendor requests are entered by the users, they will show up here in the **Vendor requests** form. Click on the new vendor request that you just entered.

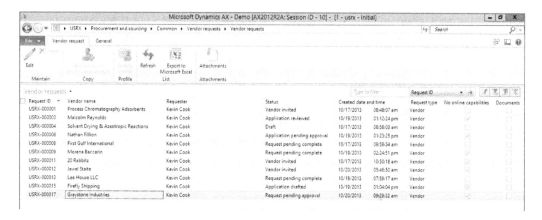

You are able to update any of the information associated with the **New Vendor Request**, and you can approve it just by clicking on the **Actions** button in the workflow toolbar, and selecting the **Approve** option.

If you want to add any comments to accompany your approval, then you can add them in the **Comments** dialog box before you click on the **Approve** button.

Note: If you want to track the progress of the workflow and any other comments associated with it, then you can always click on the **Actions** button in the workflow toolbar and select the **View history** option. This will allow you to track all of the steps that have occurred while processing this particular workflow instance.

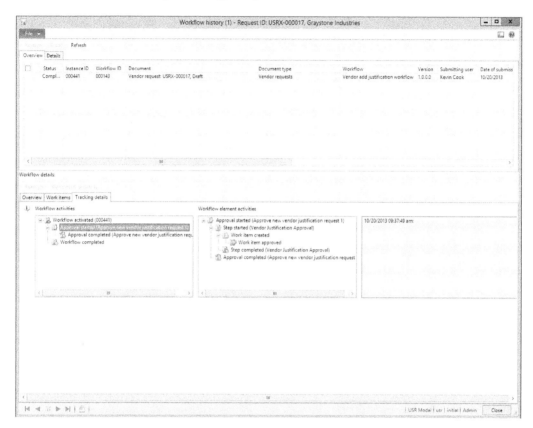

If you click the **Close** button, you will be returned to the **Vendor requests** list page, and you will see that the status of the vendor has now been changed to *Vendor Invited* which means that they are now progressing through into the vendor setup stage.

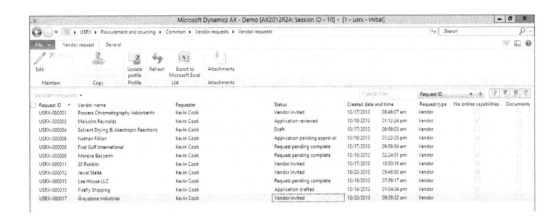

Configuring the Vendor Application Approval Workflow

Before we start the next step in the process we need to create a simple workflow for the approval of the addition of the new vendor through the vendor request.

HOW TO DO IT...

From the **Setup** group on the **Procurement and sourcing** area page, click on the **Procurement and sourcing workflows** menu item.

If you do not already have a **Vendor add application workflow** defined, click on the **New** button in the **New** group of the **Workflow** ribbon bar.

When the procurement workflow template selection dialog box is displayed, select the **Vendor add application workflow** template and click the **Create workflow** button to create the workflow shell.

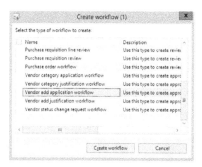

When the workflow designer is displayed, create a simple flow that just has the **Review new vendor application** step, an **Approve new vendor application** and then click on the

Save and close button to save and activate the workflow.

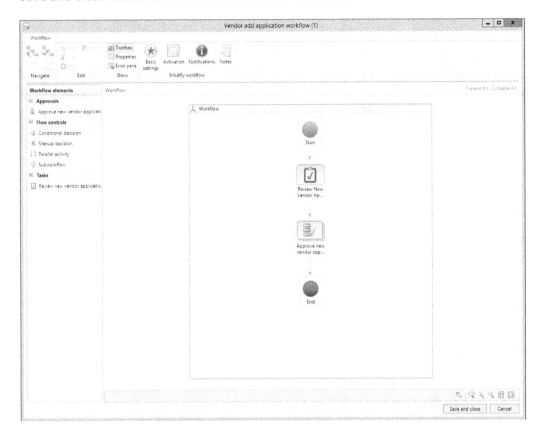

Approving New Vendor Applications

Once the vendor has been approved through the justification approval process, it moves on to the application approval process which allows the purchasing department to add the final details required for the vendor, and when it is approved will also create the new vendor record for you.

HOW TO DO IT...

To approve a new vendor application, follow these steps:

To see all of the pending vendor requests, click on the **Vendor profile pending approval** link within the **Vendor Requests** folder of the **Common** group on the **Procurement and sourcing** area page.

As new vendor requests are initially approved by the users, they will show up here in the **Vendor profile pending approval** form. Click on the new vendor request that you just entered.

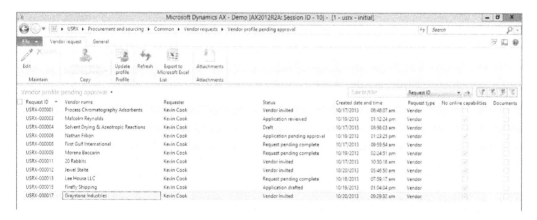

This will open up a simplified Vendor details form with the information from the vendor request. There are some fields that need to be populated still though, so click on the **Update profile** button within the **Maintain** group of the **Vendor** ribbon bar.

Fill in the required fields such as the **Vendor group** and the **Currency**, and when you have finished click the **Save** button within the **Maintain** group of the **Vendor** ribbon bar.

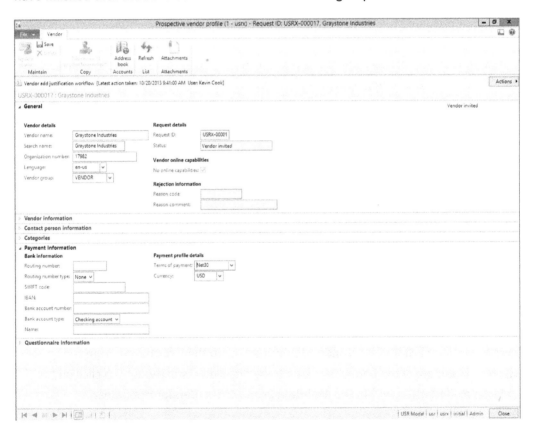

You should notice that the **Actions** button will change and now be labeled **Submit** which means that all of the necessary information has been updated in the record.

Click the **Submit** button, enter any additional comments that you want to be associated with the workflow, and then click the **Submit** button in the dialog box.

This will then notify the reviewer in the workflow that they have a new vendor request that needs to be reviewed. They are able to open up the request and from the **Actions** workflow menu item click on the **Review new vendor application** option.

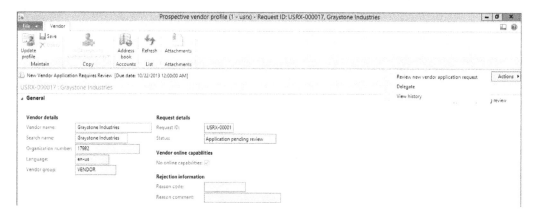

When the **Vendor application review** dialog box is displayed the reviewer is able to enter in any comments and then click the **Review new vendor application request** button to move it onto the next step in the workflow.

The final step in the workflow is to approve the vendor application. After being notified, the approver is able to open up the vendor request and from the **Actions** menu button in the workflow toolbar they can route the request back to the approver, or click on the **Approve** button to complete the vendor approval process.

The approver is then able to add any comments to the approval, and then click **Approve** to finish the process.

After the approval is completed, the status of the vendor request will change to *Application Approved* and the user is able to click the **Close** button to finish the process.

If you look at the **Vendors** tables, you will notice that there is a new vendor record that has automatically been created based of the vendor request.

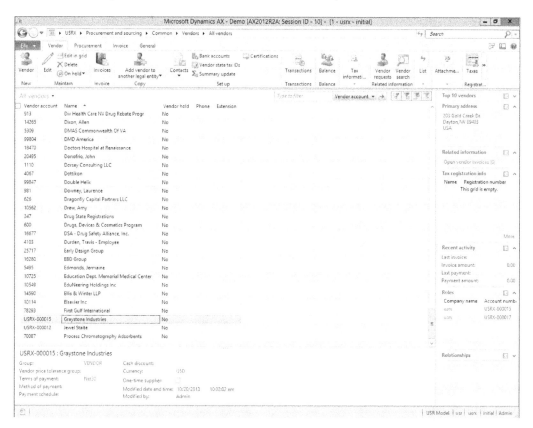

All of the information from the Vendor Request would have been copied over to the new vendor record that was created.

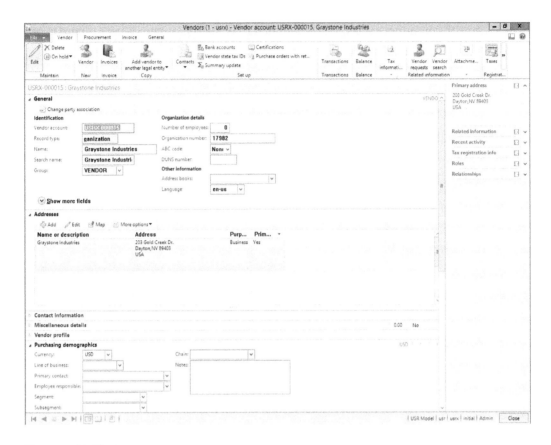

How cool is that.

Configuring the User Provisioning Request Workflow

In addition to configuring the vendors, there is also a process built into Dynamics AX that allows you to manage the provisioning of user access to the Vendor Portal, by allowing vendors to request access, and then allowing the purchasing department to approve the access and then having the system administrators provision the user.

HOW TO DO IT...

From the **Workflow** folder of the **Setup** group on the **System administration** area page, click on the **User workflows** menu item.

Double-click on the **User request workflow** workflow to open up the designer.

Configure the workflow to have a review and also an approval step within the workflow and then click the **Save and close** button to activate the workflow.

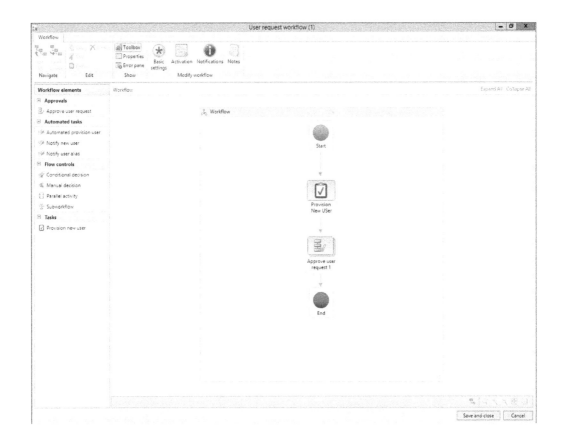

Requesting a Portal User Account for a Vendor

Once the workflow has been configured you can request user accounts to be configured for the vendors through the Procurement area.

HOW TO DO IT...

Click on the **Vendor user requests** menu item within the **Vendor requests** folder of the **Common** group of the **Procurement and sourcing** area page.

When the **Vendor user requests** list page is displayed, click on the **Add vendor user** button within the **New** group of the **Requests** ribbon bar.

When the **User request details** form is displayed, select the **Vendor account**, **Person**, and also specify a **User alias** for the request and press CTRL-S to save the record.

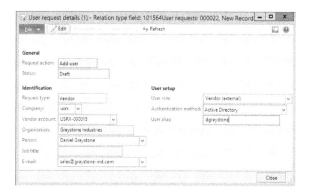

Once all of the required fields are entered, the **Submit** button will be displayed on the workflow toolbar. Click it to kick of the user provisioning workflow.

When the workflow comments dialog box is displayed, enter any notes that you want to accompany the workflow and then click the **Submit** button.

Finally, click on the **Close** button to exit out of the **User Request Details** form.

Configuring a new Vendor Portal User Account

Once a new vendor user request has been submitted, then it will start the **User request workflow** to co-ordinate the setup and approval of the records.

HOW TO DO IT...

Once a new vendor user request has been submitted, if the user is involved in the approval process then they will receive notifications through all of the channels that you have associated with the workflow, including the notification list and also the pop-up notifications through the tool bar.

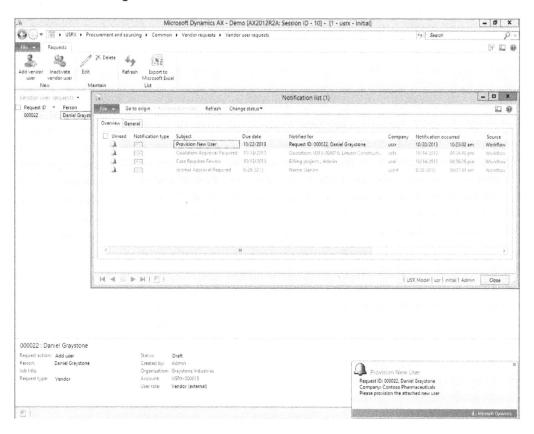

The system administrator will be able to see all of the user's details within the **Vendor user requests** maintenance form.

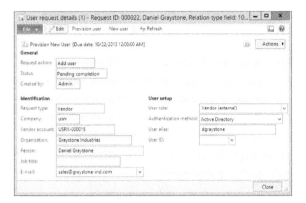

In my system I am using Active Directory authentication, so the first step is to open up the **Active Directory Users and Computers** console, and click on the **Add New User** icon in the ribbon bar.

Then create a new user for the Vendor contact.

After you have created the new user account, close down the **Active Directory Users and Computers** console.

Now we need to add the vendor as a user within Dynamics AX. To do this, click on the **Users** menu item in the **Users** folder of the **Common** group in the **System administration** area page.

Since the user is already in Active Directory, click on the **Import** button within the **New** group of the **Users** ribbon bar.

Search for the Active Directory user, check it, and then click **Next**, accepting all of the defaults for the user until the user account has been created.

Once the user account has been created, open up the record, and then click on the **Relations** button in the **Setup** group of the **User** ribbon bar.

When the **User Relations** form is displayed, click on the **New** menu button to create a new relation.

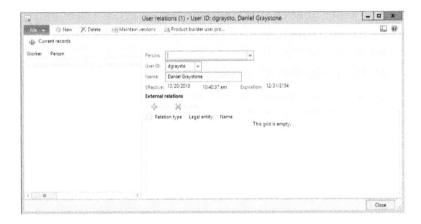

Select the vendor contact from the **Person** drop down list.

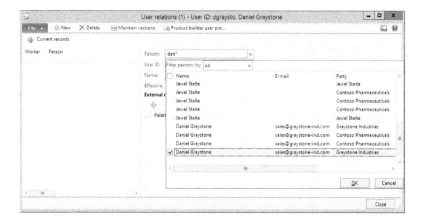

Then add a relation of type **Vendor** to the new vendor record that we created.

Click the **Close** button to exit out of the form.

Then click on the **Assign roles** button within the **User roles** tab. Select the **Vendor (external)** role, and click the **OK** button.

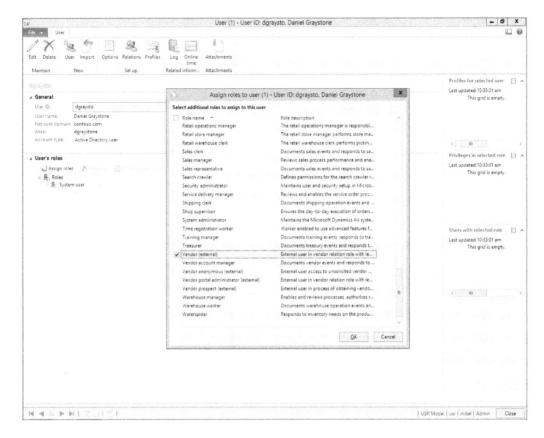

After the Vendor user is configured, click on the **Close** button to exit out of the maintenance form.

Now from the **User request details** form, you can move the workflow to the next step by select the **Complete** option within the **Actions** workflow menu button.

If you have any comments then you can enter them in, otherwise just click on the **Complete** button to finish the task.

Now that the user setup is complete, the approver will be notified that they have a pending approval task.

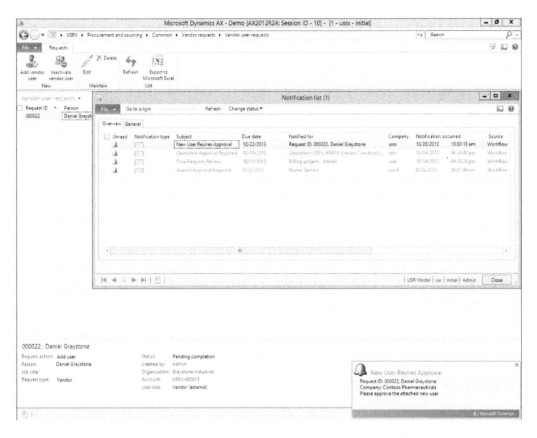

If they open up the **User request details** form for the new user request, they can approve the update just by clicking on the **Approve** option within the **Actions** workflow menu.

If they have any comments then you can enter them in, otherwise just click on the **Approve** button to finish the approval.

If you look at the **Vendor users requests** the status of the user setup should now say **Completed**.

Now the vendor is able to log into the Vendor Portal using the credentials that they were assigned by the systems administrator and access all of their information.

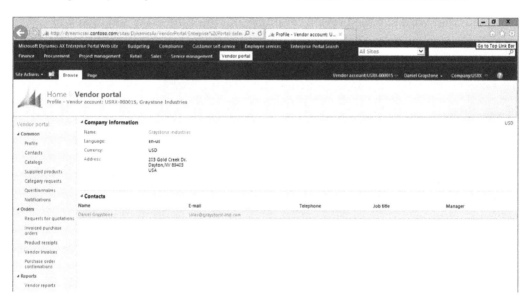

Very cool.

Allowing Prospective Vendors to Update Their Information

There is one final area that we will describe in this walkthrough that allows the Prospective Vendors to be involved in the setup process even before they are approved vendors. This allows the Prospective vendors to update their proposed vendor details themselves and double check vendor classifications etc.

HOW TO DO IT...

To include Prospective Vendors in the vendor approval process, create the vendor request just like we did in the previous example, but this time make sure that you uncheck the **No online capabilities** checkbox.

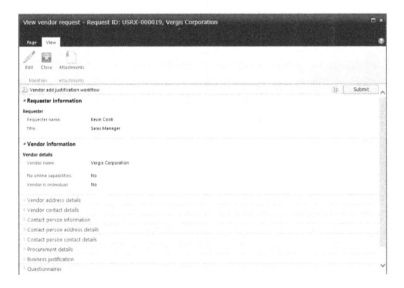

After the vendor has gone through the justification approval process, the system administrator will be notified that there is a new user request pending for the prospective vendor.

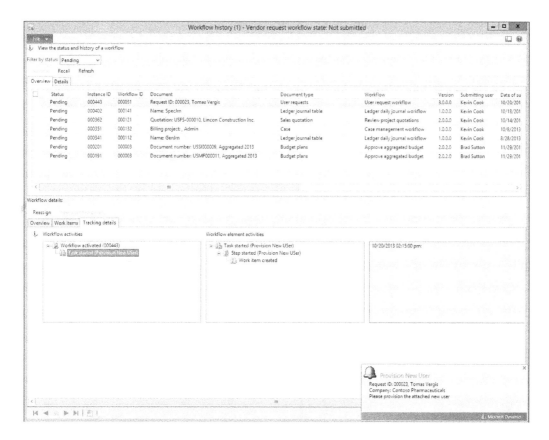

To see the request, click on the **Prospective vendor user requests** menu item within the **Vendor requests** folder of the **Common** group in the **Procurement and sourcing** area page.

From there you will see the new prospective vendor user request.

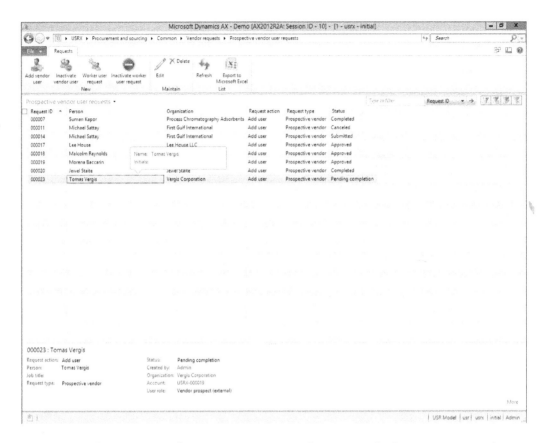

You just need to provision the new user account almost exactly the same way as the Vendor User account was set up in the previous section, except link the record to a **Prospective vendor** relation and assign it the **Vendor prospect (external)** role.

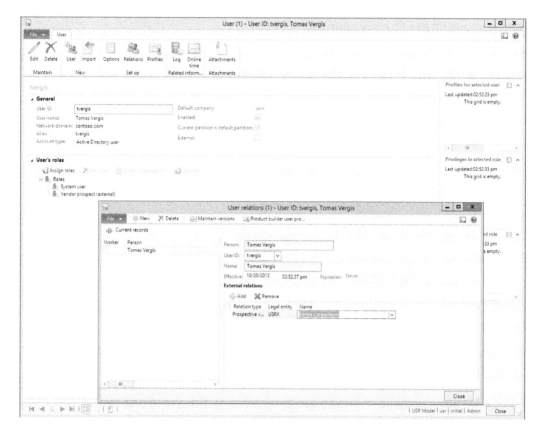

When it's finished, click on the **Complete** option from the **Actions** workflow menu button.

If they have any comments then you can enter them in, otherwise just click on the

Complete button to finish the approval.

Then the approver will be notified of the setup request and they are able to click on the **Approve** menu option of the **Actions** workflow menu button to complete the process.

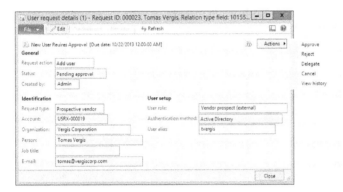

If they have any comments then you can enter them in, otherwise just click on the **Approve** button to finish the approval.

Once you have completed the process, the Prospective Vendor User Request should have the status **Completed**.

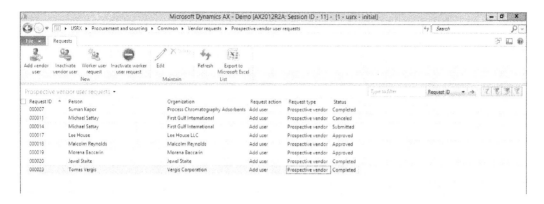

This will allow the prospective vendor to log into the Enterprise portal, and access the **Prospective vendor registration** form with all of the information from the Vendor request.

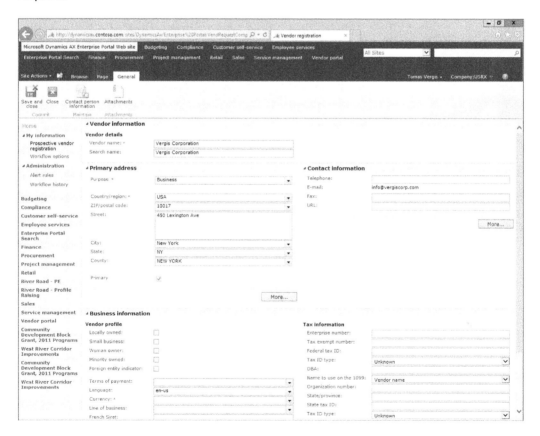

They are able to update any of their details, and also need to confirm the **Category information** that has been associated with their prospective vendor account.

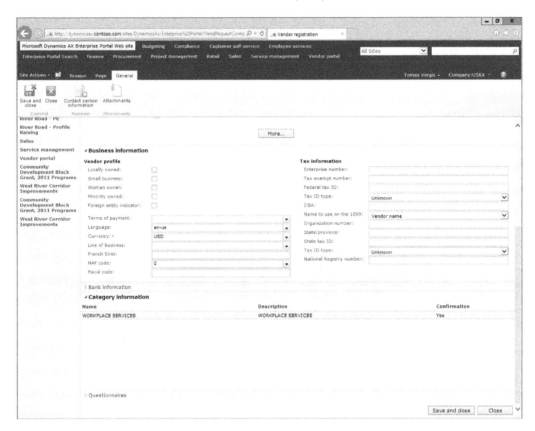

Note: They also have access to the **Attachments** functionality, so if they want to give you any other associated documentation, then they can do that from here as well.

Once they have done that, the **Submit** button will be displayed in the workflow toolbar, and they can mark the vendor as being updated and ready for approval.

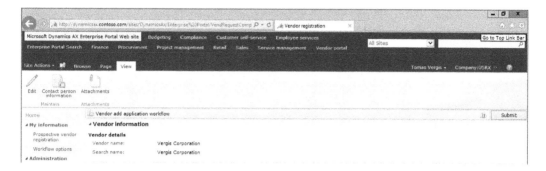

They can add any notes to the submission if they like and then click the **Submit** button.

Once they have submitted their profile, they can exit from the form.

After the prospective vendor has returned the information, then the reviewing process will run just like it did in the prior example.

Summary

The vendor on-boarding process makes the setting up of vendors so much easier, especially when you have multiple people involved in the setup and approval process.

In this example we have just shown a couple of the options that are available to you. Once you have mastered the basics, you can try the following:

- Adding questionnaires for gathering additional information from the vendors during on-boarding
- Tweaking the vendor justification options
- Automating the user setup process workflows
- Adding multiple routings and approval steps for the workflow processes.

This is not going to be everyone's cup of tea, and may be overkill for some of you, but for those that do have more formal processes in place for adding vendors, this will definitely be a life saver and allow you to manage the on-boarding process a lot more effectively. Give it a go, I'm sure it will be worth the setup.

Configuring Vendor Ratings & Scorecards

Dynamics AX allows you to configure your own **Vendor Evaluation Criteria** and then track the vendor performance against any or all of the criteria that you have defined. When you combine this with the Power BI tools, you get a great way to rate vendors, and also a nice way to present Vendor Scorecards.

In this worked example we will show how to configure the Vendor Evaluations, and also how to create a simple Vendor Scorecard without breaking a sweat.

Creating Vendor Evaluation Criteria Groups

The first step in configuring the **Vendor Ratings** within Dynamics AX is to create some **Vendor Evaluation Criteria Groups**. These will be used to group common sets of evaluation criteria together and allow you to get summary results on the evaluations at the criteria group level.

HOW TO DO IT...

Select the **Vendor evaluation criteria group** menu item from the **Vendors** folder of the **Setup** group on the **Procurement and sourcing** area page.

When the maintenance form for the **Vendor evaluation criteria groups** is displayed, click on the **New** button on the menu bar to add a new record.

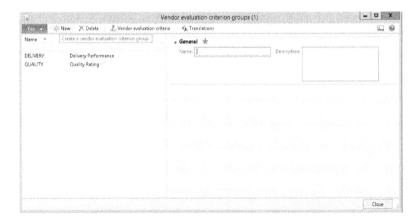

Enter your Criteria Group code in the **Name** field and a brief description in the **Description** field.

After creating any other **Vendor Evaluation Criteria Groups** in the maintenance form, click the **Close** button to exit.

Creating Vendor Evaluation Criteria

Once you have set up your **Vendor Evaluation Criteria Groups**, you will need to set up some **Vendor Evaluation Criteria** codes that you will use to rate your vendors.

HOW TO DO IT...

Select the **Vendor evaluation criteria** menu item from the **Vendors** folder of the **Setup** group on the **Procurement and sourcing** area page.

When the maintenance form for the **Vendor evaluation criteria** is displayed, click on the **New** button on the menu bar to add a new record.

Enter your Criteria code in the **Name** field, a brief description in the **Description** field, and select the **Vendor evaluation criteria group** that you want the evaluation criteria to be associated with.

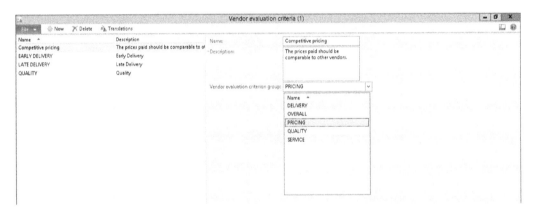

After creating any other **Vendor Evaluation Criteria** in the maintenance form, click the **Close** button to exit.

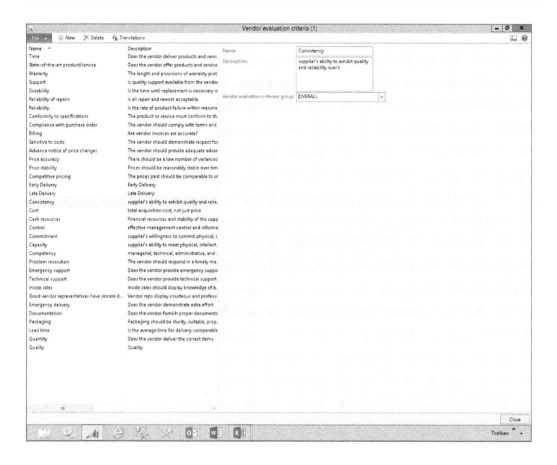

Configuring Vendors for Evaluation

The final step in the setup process is to link the **Evaluation Criteria** with the **Vendors** within Dynamics AX. This is done through the **Procurement Categories**.

HOW TO DO IT...

Select the **Procurement categories** menu item from the **Categories** folder of the **Setup** group on the **Procurement and sourcing** area page.

Within the **Procurement categories** maintenance form select the top level node of your **Categories** and then open up the **Vendor evaluation criteria groups** tab within the detail area.

To associate your **Vendor Evaluation criteria groups** click on the **Add** button in the tabs menu bar.

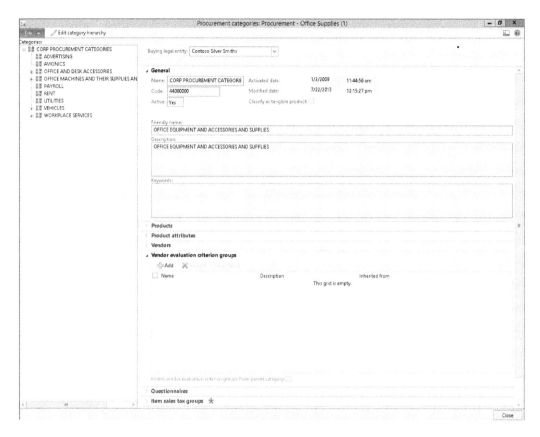

Select all of the **Evaluation Criteria Groups** that you want the vendors to be measured on, and click on the **Select** button to add them to the selection box.

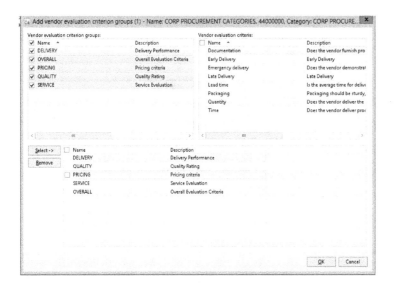

Once you have finished, click the **OK** button to return to the main form.

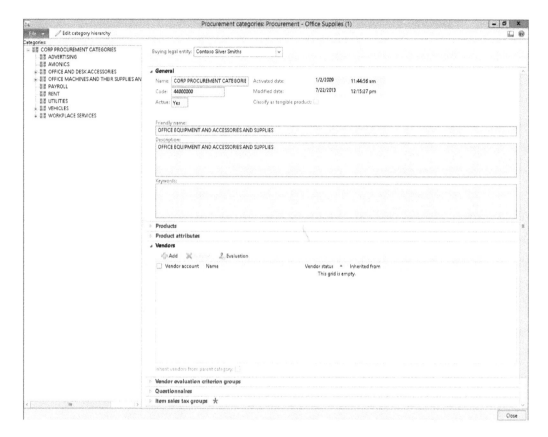

Now all of the **Vendor Evaluation Criteria Groups** should be associated with your procurement category.

This will open up a Vendor Selection form. Select all of the vendors that you want to include in the evaluations, and click on the **Select** button to add them to the selection list.

When you are finished, click on the **OK** button to return to the main form.

You can continue this process for any of the leaf nodes in the Procurement Hierarchy.

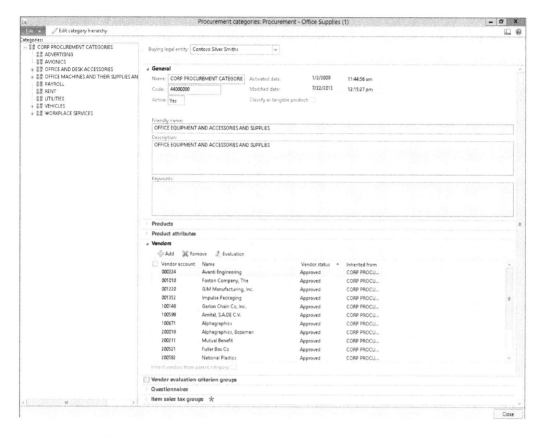

When you are finished, click on the **Close** button to exit from the form.

Recording Vendor Evaluations

Once the evaluation criteria have been configured, you can start recording the vendor ratings.

HOW TO DO IT...

Select the Procurement categories menu item from the Categories folder of the **Setup** group on the **Procurement and sourcing** area page, and expand the **Vendors** tab.

Select the vendor that you want to record the evaluations against and click on the **Evaluations** button in the menu bar.

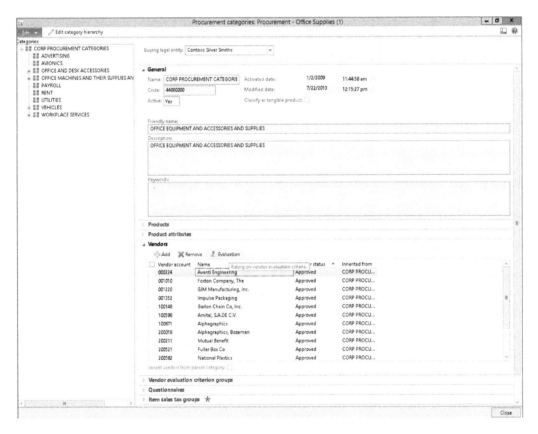

This will open up the **Ratings** maintenance form with all of the **Evaluation Criteria**

Groups listed on the left, and all of the **Evaluation Criteria** for that group on the right.

To update any of the vendor ratings, just select the rating for the criteria that you want to update and select the rating that you would like to apply.

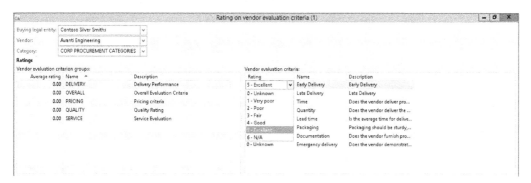

Continue this process for all of the evaluation criteria that you want to report on.

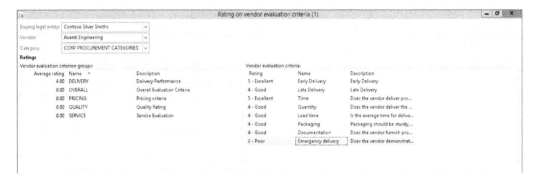

Notice that the **Average Rating** for the **Evaluation Criteria Group** will change as you enter in the results.

Repeat this for all of the **Criteria Evaluation Groups**.

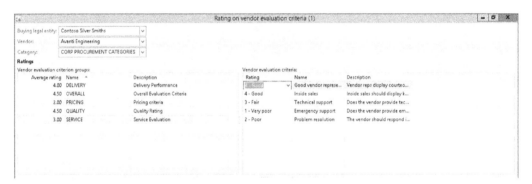

Once you have finished, you can just click **Close** to exit out of the form.

Creating a Vendor Evaluation Scorecard through Power BI

Now that you have all of the vendor ratings recorded within Dynamics AX, you will probably want to generate a vendor evaluation scorecard. Rather than having a static report, why not do this through Power BI, and create some interactive dashboards that you can drill around in.

HOW TO DO IT...

Start off by opening Excel, and from the **Dynamics AX** ribbon bar, select the **Add Data** option from the **Design** group.

Filter out the tables to just the ones that begin with **VendReview*** and select the following tables:

VendReviewCriterionGroupRating

VendReviewCriterionRating

Then click on the **OK** button to add the tables to your spreadsheet.

Select the VendReviewCriterionGroupRating tab that is created and add the **Average rating** field to the spreadsheet.

Select the VendReviewCriterionRating tab that is created and add the **Rating** field to the spreadsheet.

Click on the **Fields** button within the **Design** group of the **Dynamics AX** ribbon bar to return to data mode.

Then select the **Refresh** button in the **Data** group of the **Dynamics AX** ribbon bar, and select the **Refresh All** option.

Now you will be able to see all of the overall ratings for the vendors that you entered into Dynamics AX.

And within the other tab you will be able to see all of the detailed ratings.

Now we need to link the two tables through Power Pivot. To do this, select the **POWERPIVOT** ribbon bar and click on the **Manage** button within the **Data Model** group.

This will open up a blank Power Pivot canvas.

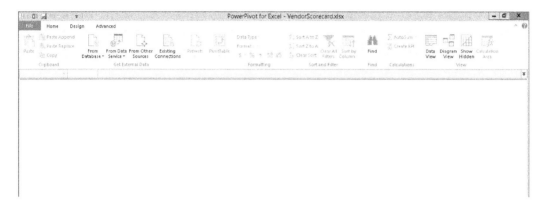

Return to the spreadsheet and select the **VenReviewCriterionGroupRating** sheet and click on the **Add to Data Model** button within the **Tables** group of the **POWERPIVOT** ribbon bar.

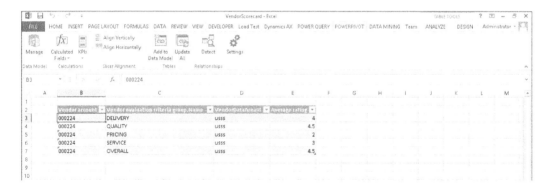

This will add the table to the Power Pivot model.

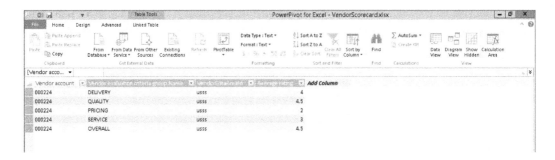

Return to the spreadsheet and select the **VenReviewCriterionRating** sheet and click on the **Add to Data Model** button within the **Tables** group of the **POWERPIVOT** ribbon bar.

Now both tables will be within the model.

From the **View** group of the **Home** ribbon bar, select the **Diagram View** menu to switch to the diagram version of the editor.

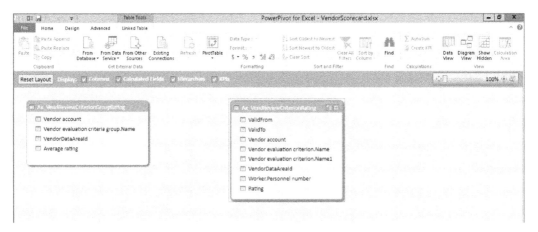

Then select the **Vendor evaluation criteria group.Name** field within the **Ax_VendReviewCriterionGroupRating** table, and drag it over to the **Vendor evaluation criteria.Name1** field within the **Ax_VendReviewCriterionRating** table to link the two tables.

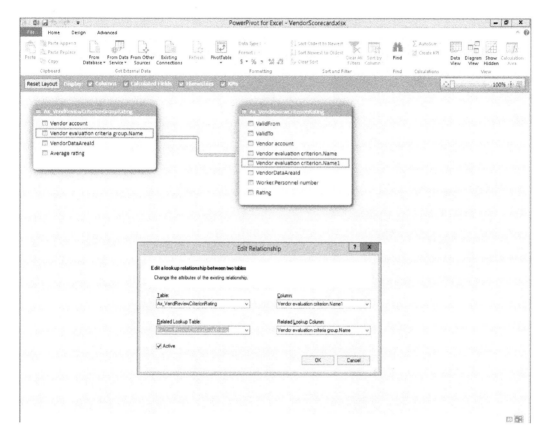

Once you have done that, you can close down the **Power Pivot Model** window and return to Excel.

Now we will start creating the Vendor Scorecard within Power View. To do this, select the **Insert** ribbon bar within Excel, and click on the **Power View** button within the **Reports** group.

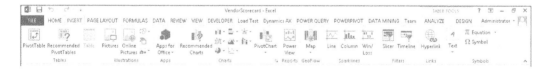

This will create a new worksheet within Excel with a **Power View** report embedded within it.

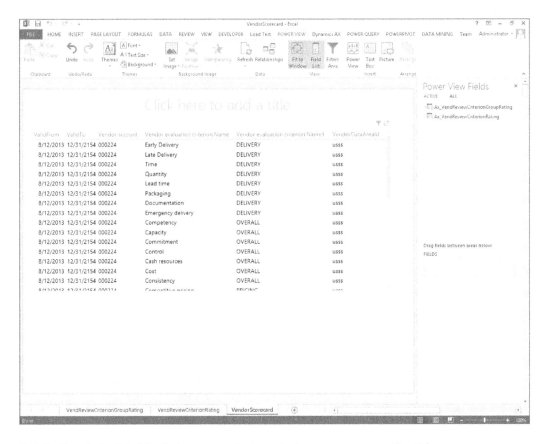

Delete the default table that was created, and give your scorecard a title.

Create a data panel for the Vendor.

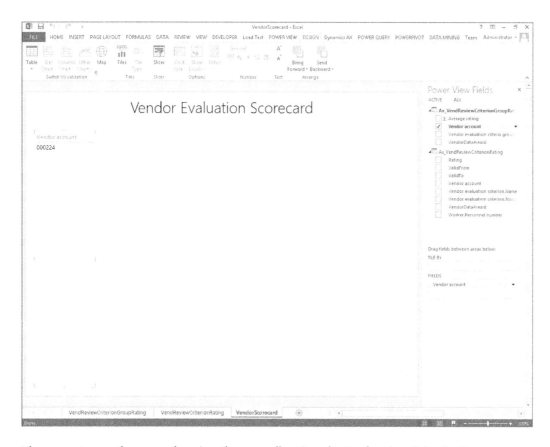

Then create another one showing the overall ratings by **Evaluation Criteria Group**.

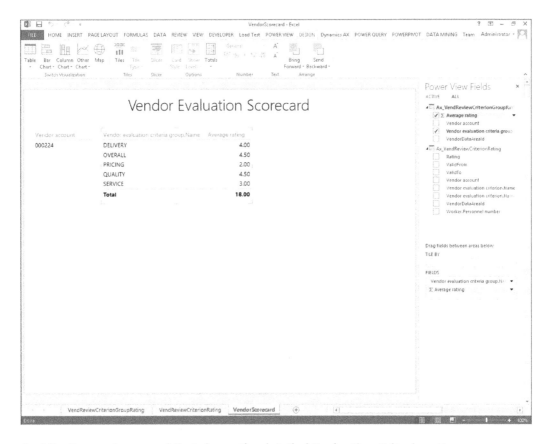

And finally, create a panel that shows the detailed **Evaluation Criteria** ratings.

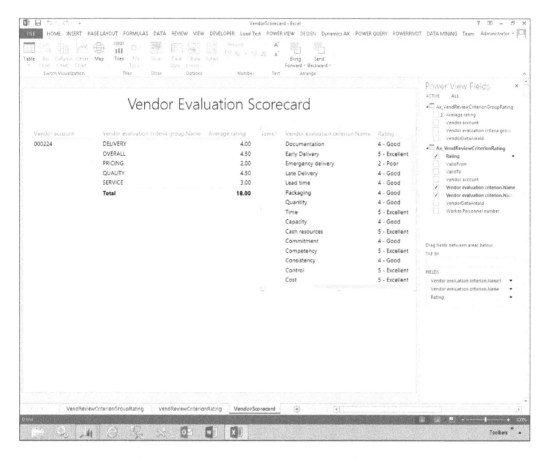

Now convert the Evaluation Criteria Group Ratings to a column chart.

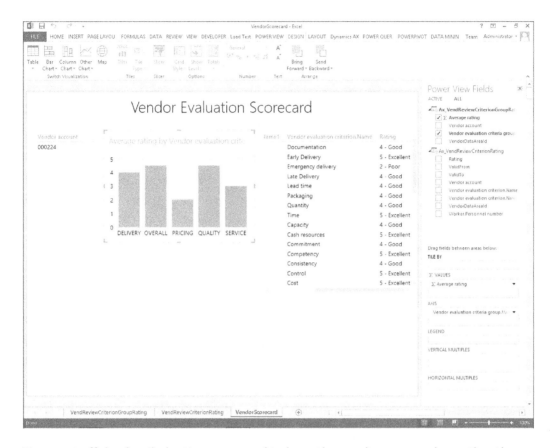

To report off the detailed ratings, we need to have the results as a number rather than the text selection that is used by default. To do this, open up the **Power Pivot Model** and create a new column called **RatingValue** on the **VendReviewCriterionRating** table.

Set the field to be the left most character of the rating, and then change the data type to be a number.

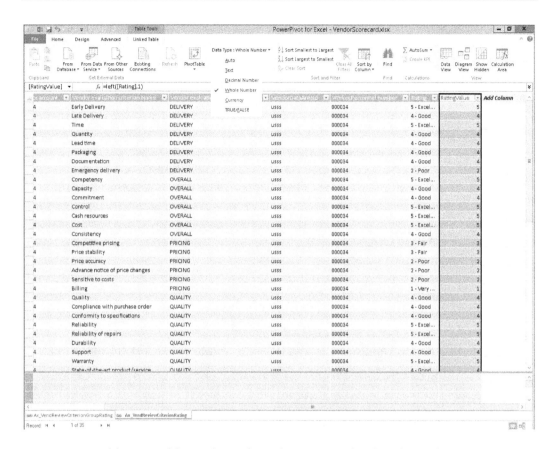

Now we can add some additional panels to the scorecard to break out the results.

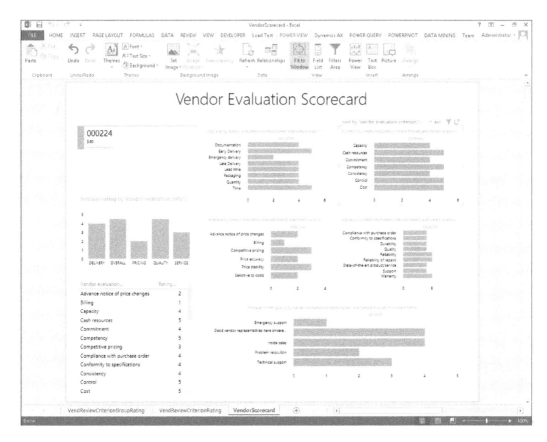

Selecting any particular evaluation criteria group will allow you to highlight different areas of the evaluation detail.

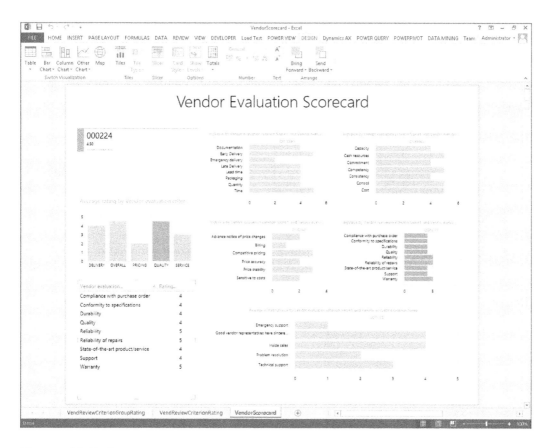

How cool is that.

Summary

In this example we have shown how to set up the **Vendor Evaluation Criteria** within Dynamics AX, and then use that data to create a simple **Vendor Evaluation Scorecard**.

This is just the starting point. Once you have mastered this, you may want to:

- Add date ranges to your scorecard. Dynamics AX will track all of the changes to the Vendor Ratings through effectivity dates.

- Push ratings automatically to the rating system through API's

- Create a vendor rating entry form in InfoPath to make it even easier to update the ratings.

This isn't too bad for an out-of-the-box function, and a little bit of Excel reporting

Setting Up A Retail Store With POS

Dynamics AX 2012 now has a retail module that includes store management, and also the ability to set up Retail Point of Sales (POS) terminals to take orders, manage store inventory and also track customers. It may seem a little bit daunting to set up, but it's really not that hard.

In this blueprint we will go through all of the steps that are required for you to set up your first retail store and then configure the POS register so that you can take orders through the touch screens.

Set Retail Store Number Sequence To Manual

Before you start I would make one small suggestion for your system. And that is to change the numbering sequence on the Store and Register ID's to be manual. This is an entirely optional step, but having a store code and also a register code that is easy to read directly from the screen will make the process a little easier.

HOW TO DO IT...

To do this, open up the **Retail Shared Parameters** menu from the **Parameters** folder of the **Setup** group on the **Retail** area page.

Select the **Number sequences** group in the parameters.

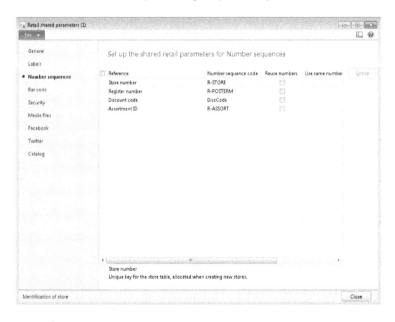

Right-mouse click on the **Number sequence code** field for the *Store number* to open up the context menu, and select the **View Details** option to access the number sequence details.

When the number sequence definition is displayed, click on the **Edit** button in the **Maintain** group of the **Number Sequence** ribbon bar to enter into edit mode.

In the **General** group, click on the **Manual** check box to enable manual numbering. Then click close to save the number sequence.

Now repeat the process for the *Register number*. Right-mouse click on the **Number sequence code** field for the *Register number* to open up the context menu, and select the **View Details** option to access the number sequence details.

When the number sequence definition is displayed, click on the **Edit** button in the **Maintain** group of the **Number Sequence** ribbon bar to enter into edit mode. In the **General** group, click on the **Manual** check box to enable manual numbering. Then click close to save the number sequence.

Create A Store Warehouse

Before we set up the Store, we need to quickly create a Warehouse that we will use to manage the store inventory. This will be replenished from our main warehouses, but will allow the store managers and users to use the POS system for cycle counts, and also allow all of the organization to view the available inventory separated out by store.

HOW TO DO IT...

Open up the **Warehouses** menu item from the **Inventory breakdown** folder of the **Setup** group on the **Inventory and warehouse management** area page.

From the **Warehouses** form, click on the **New** button to create a new Warehouse record.

Give your Warehouse a code and a name. In this example, to make things easier to link up, I have used the city name as the Warehouse code. Then assign the warehouse to a **Site**, and if you are using **Quarantine** and **Transit** warehouses then register those against the new warehouse as well.

In the **Master Planning** section, check the **Refilling** check box, and select a **Main Warehouse**. This will designate the warehouse that is going to be used to supply your store for planning purposes.

In the **Location names** group, configure your location types and numbering sequences. For my warehouse I am going to create Aisles and Racks for the store. I don't think we need much more than that for our example.

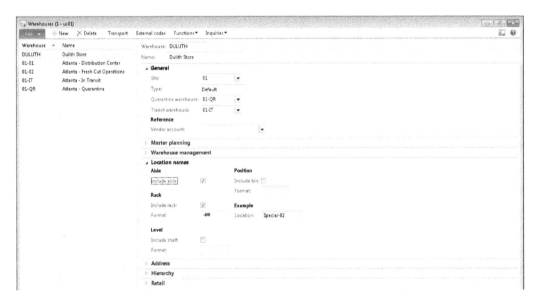

Now we need to create the Inventory Locations. We could copy these from an existing warehouse, but since we don't have any currently configured, we will use the **Location**

Wizard that you will be able to access from the **Functions** menu to help us built the locations.

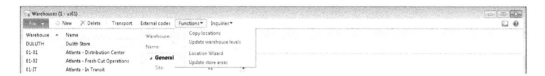

When the **Location Wizard** form shows up, just click **Next** through the Welcome screen.

Check all of the option boxed for the **Location Types** and then click **Next**.

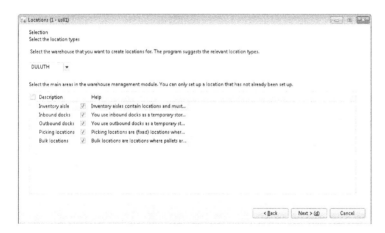

Select the number of *Special Aisles* that you want in your Store Warehouse. In this example, we just want 1.

Click **Next** to confirm the suggested Inventory Aisles.

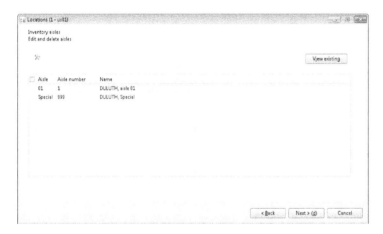

Now select the number of **Inbound Docks** for the Store. We will just have 1 for ours. Then click **Next**.

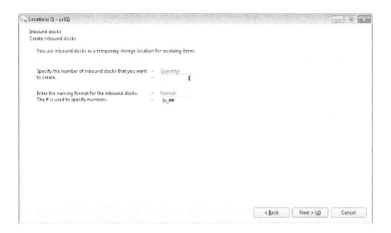

Click **Next** to confirm the suggested Inbound Docks.

Now select the number of **Outbound Docks** for the Store. We will just have 1 for ours. Then click **Next**.

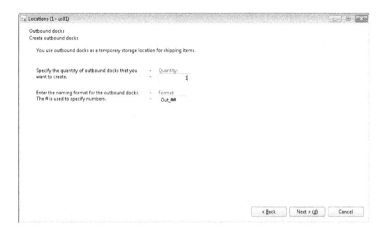

Click **Next** to confirm the suggested Outbound Docks.

Now select the configuration of your Aisles and Racks for the **Picking Locations**. This form will change based on your Warehouse location configuration. For this example. We will just create one Aisle with 5 Racks for the inventory. Then click **Next**.

If you want you can specify the physical dimensions for the picking locations racks, and also the default picking locations. After doing that click **Next** to continue on.

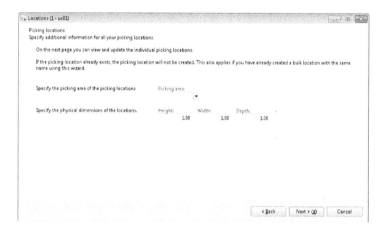

Click **Next** to confirm the suggested Picking Locations.

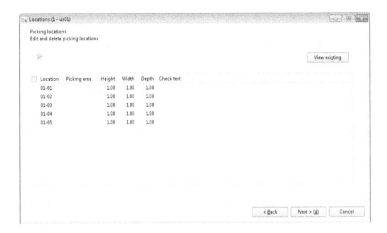

Now select the configuration of your Aisles and Racks for the **Bulk Locations**. This form will change based on your Warehouse location configuration. For this example. We will just create one Aisle with 5 Racks for the inventory. Then click **Next**.

If you want you can specify the physical dimensions for the bulk locations racks, and also the default picking locations. After doing that click **Next** to continue on.

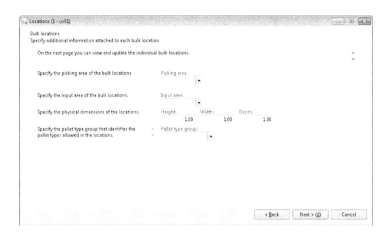

Click **Next** to confirm the suggested Bulk Locations.

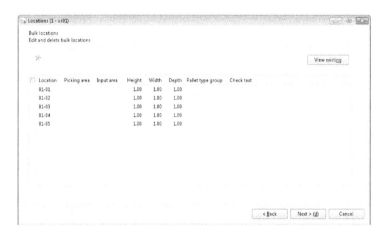

Now that the locations for your Store Warehouse have been created, you can configure your **Warehouse management** group with the default locations.

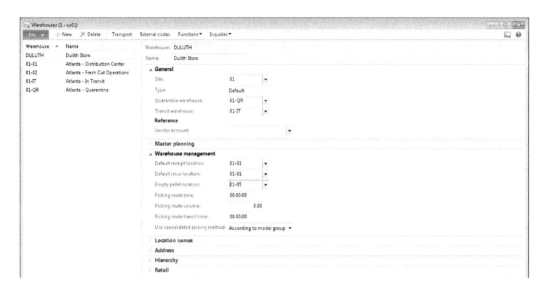

Finally, we will just need to go to the **Retail** group on the **Warehouse** record and check the **Store** checkbox to mark the warehouse as a Store Warehouse.

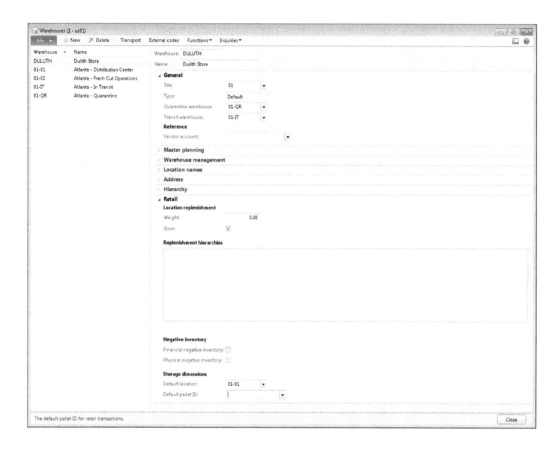

Create a Retail Store

In order to start selling via the Retail Channels, we need to create a **Store** to sell through. The Store will be associated with warehoused for stocking, customer address books for sales, and also employee groups to manage who can work at the store and their permissions. Also, later on we will be able to attach POS Registers to the stores so that we can access all of the store information and transactions through a disconnected session, and synchronize with the store later on.

HOW TO DO IT...

To access the **Store** details, open up the **Retail stores** menu item from the **Retail channels** folder of the **Common** group on the **Retail** Area page.

To create a new **Store** click on the **Retail Store** button in the **New** group of the **Store** ribbon bar.

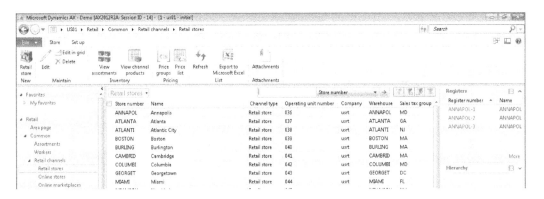

This will create a new blank **Store** record for you. If you are not already in edit mode, click on the **Edit** button in the **Maintain** group of the **Setup** ribbon bar group.

Give your new **Store** a **Name,** and **Store Number.** For our examples, we will continue to use the same naming convention that we used for the **Warehouse** and use the city name for the store name and code to make it easier to locate. Also, we can link the **Store** record to the stores **Warehouse**.

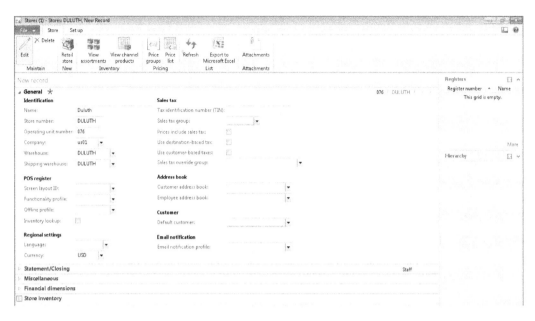

In the **POS register** section, pick a default **Screen layout ID, Functionality profile**, and also **Offline profile**. Later on we will show how you can create your own screen layouts and profiles, but for now we will use the standard layouts delivered with the system.

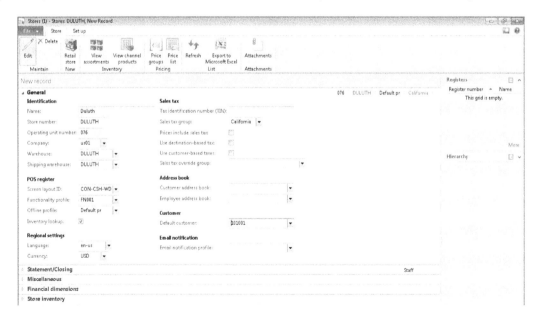

Now we will associate the **Store** record with a **Customer** and **Employee address book**. The **Employee address book** is the most important of the two, because it will allow you to link the Employees that can use the POS system to the store. Since this is a new **Store** we will create a new address book for the store. Right click on either of the address book fields, and select the **View details** option to open up the **Address Book** maintenance forms.

To create a new **Address Book**, click on the **New** button on the **Address book** maintenance form.

Then create a new address book record. Keeping with our naming conventions we're using, we will give the **Address Book** record the same name as the **Store**. After you have done this, close down the form and return to the Store record.

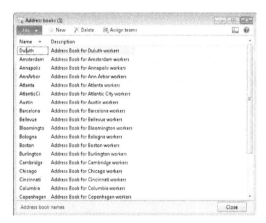

Now you can associate the **Store** record with an address book for the customers, and also the employees.

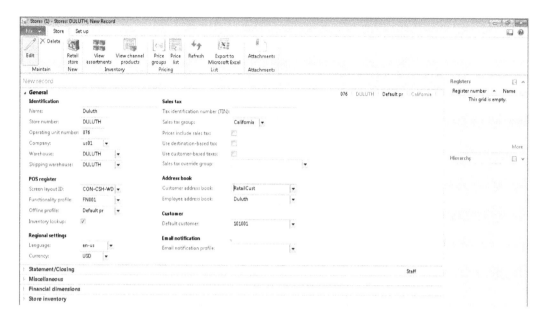

In the **Statement/Closing** section of the **Store** definition, you may want to associate rounding and difference parameters that are allowed by the store.

In the **Miscellaneous** section of the store definition, you may also want to turn off the **Hide training mode** option. This will only show up on the POS register, which we will set up later.

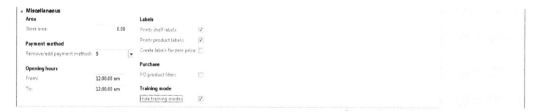

In the **Financial dimensions** section we can set the default dimensions for the store.

The final step in the process is to set up all of the payment methods, shift definitions, cash declarations tec. For the store. Rather than do this by hand, you can save time by clicking on the **Copy all** menu button from the **Copy** Group of the **Setup** ribbon bar.

This will allow you to select another Store record to copy all of the miscellaneous settings from.

After you have done that you can click on the **Close** button to save the **Store** definition.

Adding Store to a Retail Channel

After creating a **Store** there is a small housekeeping step that needs to be performed. And that is to add the **Store** to the **Organizational Hierarchies**. Later on we will use this as we are defining the **Product Assortments** to assign valid sellable products to stores.

HOW TO DO IT...

Access the **Organizational Hierarchy** details, open up the **Organizational hierarchies** menu item from the **Organization** folder of the **Setup** group on the **Organization administration** Area page.

From the **Organization hierarchies** form you will be able o see the retail hierarchies that are defined. For each of these we will probably want to add our new **Store**. To do this, select the hierarchy that you want to maintain, and click on the **View** button in the menu bar.

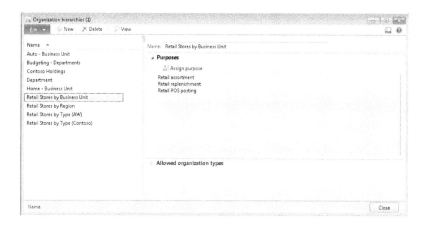

This will open up a hierarchical view explorer. To edit the hierarchy click on the **Edit** button from the **Maintain** group of the **View hierarchy** ribbon bar. This will swap you into edit mode.

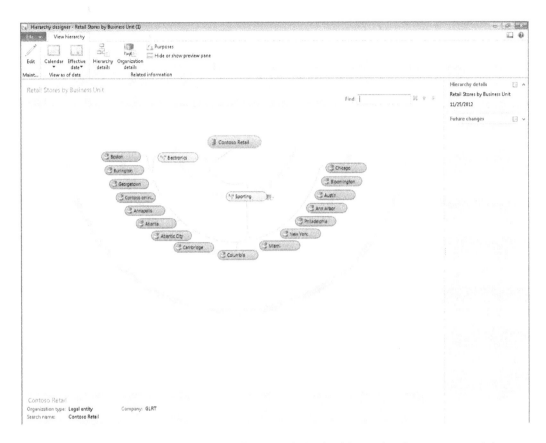

If you don not currently have your **Business Unit** in the hierarchy then you can right-click on the parent node and select the **Business Unit** option from the **Insert** menu item.

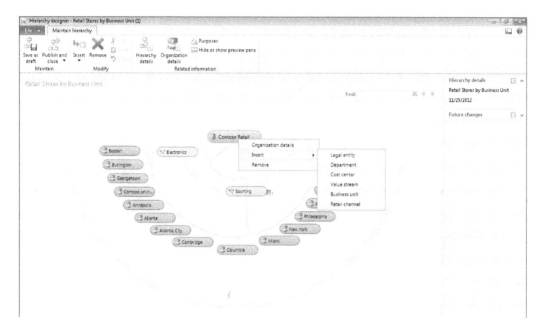

This will allow you to browse through the un0used business units and add them to the hierarchy.

To add your new **Store** to the **Retail hierarchy**, right mouse click on the **Business Unit** that you want to add it to and select the **Retail channel** option from the **Insert** menu group.

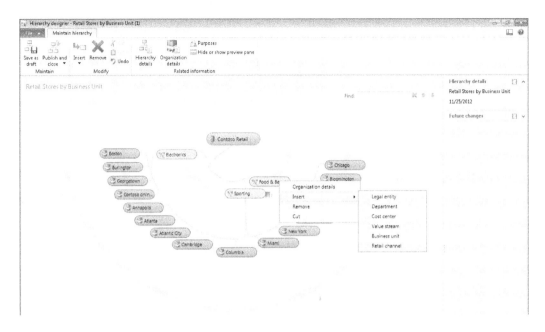

From here you will be able to see all of the **Stores** that are not currently in your hierarchy – including your new store, and you can select it and click **OK** to add it.

To activate the hierarchy, select the **Publish and close** menu button from the **Maintain** group on the **Maintain hierarchy** ribbon bar, specify an activation date for the hierarchy, and then click **Publish.**

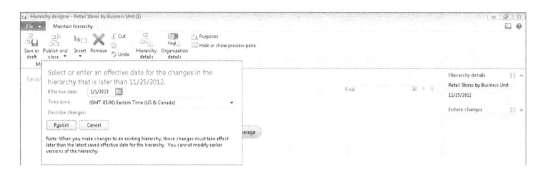

Repeat this process for any other **Retail Hierarchies** that you may have within your system.

Now you will be able to browse through the hierarchy and see your **Store.**

Configuring Workers for Retail

Once you have your **Store** configured, you will want to assign workers to them so that they will be able allowed to use the POS Registers. This is done by adding them to the stores address book, and also configuring their default Retail options.

HOW TO DO IT...

To access the **Worker** details, open up the **Workers** menu item from the **Workers** folder of the **Common** group on the **Human resources** Area page.

From the worker list, find the one that you want to assign to your store address book, and click the **Edit** button from the **Maintain** group of the **Worker** ribbon bar.

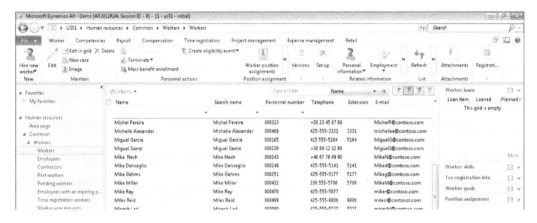

This will open up the **Worker** maintenance form. In the **Other information** group of the **Worker summary** section, select the **Address book** field, and from the multi-selection box, select the **Address Books** that you want to add the worker to. The worker may belong to multiple address books, but in order to use the POS systems in the **Store** make sure that on of them is the stores address book.

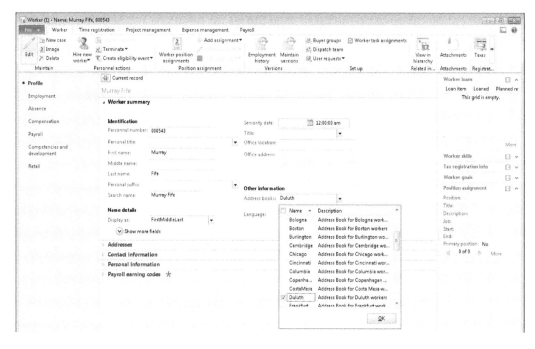

While we are in the Worker record, we might as well configure some of the other default retail options for them. To do this click on the **Retail** group on the left hand side of the **Employee** record.

If you want the user to have their own screen layout or default retail employment type, then you can set that up here. You can also assign the user their own POS password for authentication.

Just to check that the user is correctly configured, select the **Stores** link at the bottom of the **Retail** options to open up the list of valid **Stores** for the user. You should see your new store that you assigned to them in the list.

Once you have done that, your employee record is configured.

Creating Retail Position

Before a worker is able to allow Workers to use the POS Registers, they need to be assigned a Retail Position on the organization so that they have the required rights and privileges. If we don't already have an open Position for the employee, then we will need to create one.

HOW TO DO IT...

Access the **Position** details, open up the **Positions** menu item from the **Positions** folder of the **Common** group on the **Human resources** Area page.

Find an existing **Position** record to use as a template for our new **Position**, and click the **Copy position** button from the **New** group on the **Position** ribbon bar group.

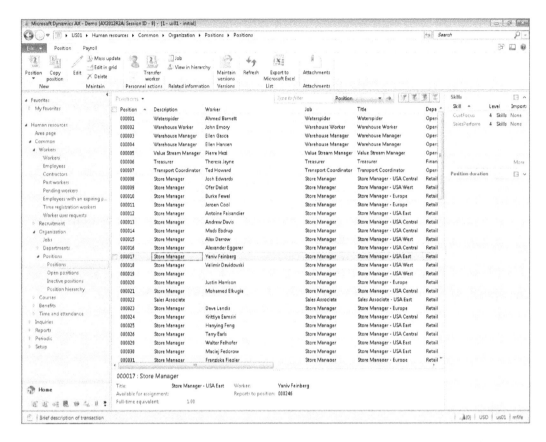

Select the number of positions that you want to create and then click the **Copy** button. In this case we just want one more *Store Manager* position.

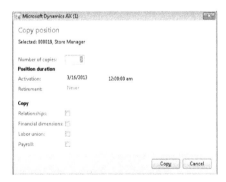

Now the system should have created a new empty **Position** record for you to use.

Assigning Workers to a Retail Position

The final step in setting up a **Worker** to allow them to use the Retail functions is to assign them to a **Retail Position**. This will assign them all of the correct rights so that they are able to access the POS Registers, and also dictate what transactions they are able to perform.

HOW TO DO IT...

Workers are assigned Positions through the **Works** maintenance form. To access the **Worker** details, open up the **Workers** menu item from the **Workers** folder of the **Common** group on the **Human resources** Area page.

Select the **Worker** record that you want to assign your **Retail Position** to.

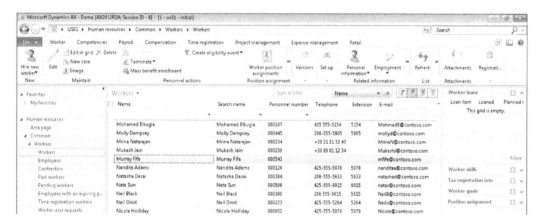

From the **Position Assignment** group on the **Worker** ribbon bar, select the **Add Assignment** button.

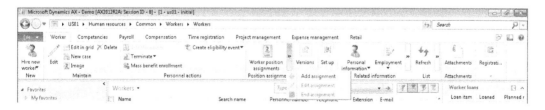

When the **Create a position assignment** dialog shows up you can select any of the open positions and assign it to your user. In this example we will make the user a Store Manager.

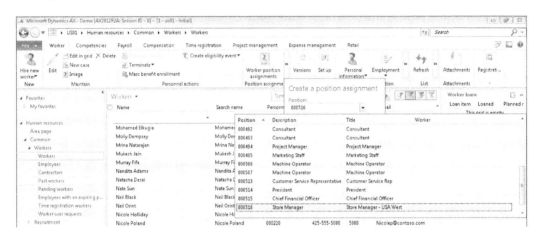

To finish the assignment of the **Position** just click on the **Create position assignment** button.

To check that the user has been assigned to your **Retail Position**, go to the **Retail** ribbon bar and click on the **POS permissions** button within the **Set up** group.

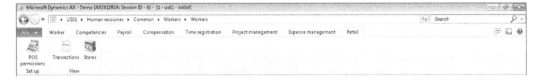

You should see the **POS position** details. This is also where you can override the default privileges associated with the position on a worker by worker basis.

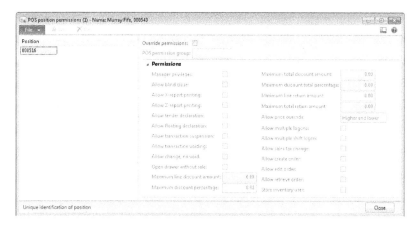

Creating New Retail Product Hierarchies

Dynamics AX allows you to organize your products into what are referred to as **Retail Product Hierarchies**, which allows you to create a tree structure of products with an unlimited number of levels and groupings. This allows you to then use these hierarchies to choose what products are to be used by the retails stores by group rather than by individual product, making the maintenance and deployment of the products much easier as you add and remove products from your catalog.

HOW TO DO IT...

Open up the **Retail product hierarchy** menu item from the **Catalog hierarchies'** folder of the **Setup** group on the **Retail** Area page.

This will open up the **Retail product hierarchy** view. To add a new section to the hierarchy, click on the **Edit category hierarchy** button in the menu bar.

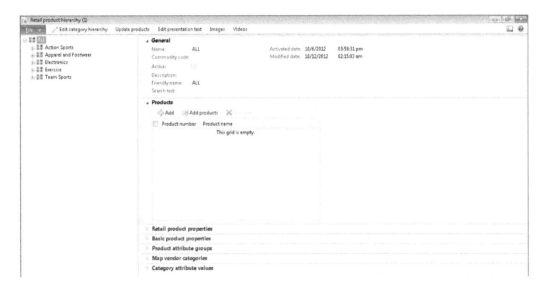

This will open up the hierarchy editor. If you are not currently in edit mode, click on the **Edit** button in the **Maintain** group of the **Category hierarchy** ribbon bar.

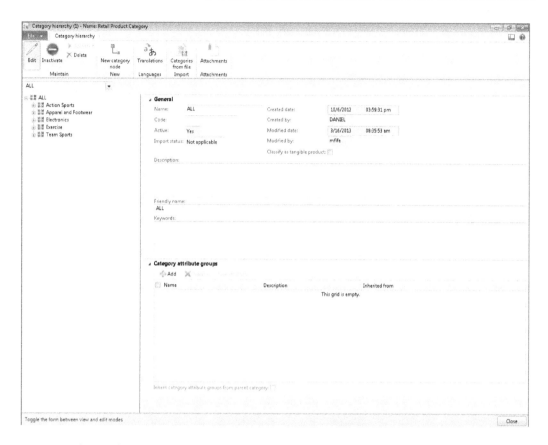

Once in edit mode, you will be able to create new structures within the hierarchy. To create a new base category, select the **ALL** node in the hierarchy tree and click on the **New category node** button in the **New** group of the **Category hierarchy** menu bar.

When the new node is created, you can assign the category node a **Name**, **Description**, **Friendly Name**, and **Keywords**.

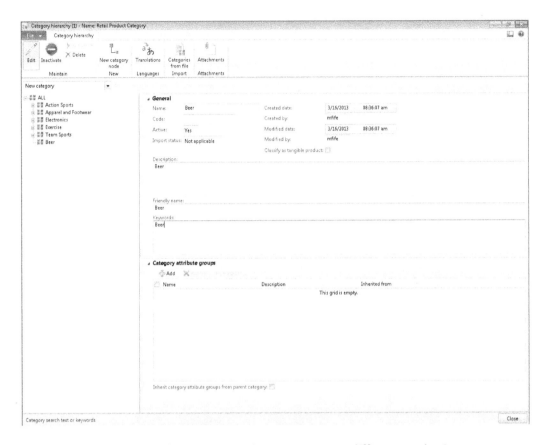

NOTE: You can continue this process and create as many different nodes in your hierarchy as you like, and also create as many levels as you like.

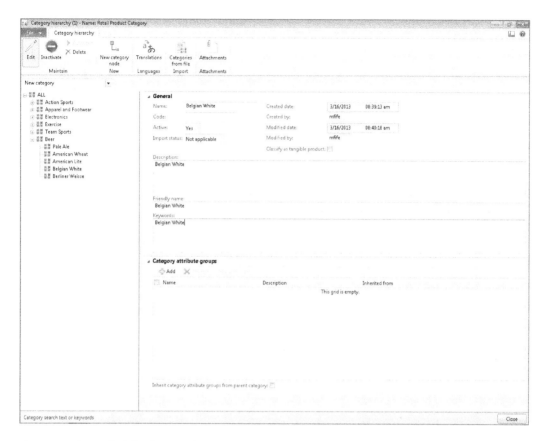

Once you have finished, just click on the **Close** button to return to the main **Retail Product Hierarchies** form.

Now you need to assign products to your hierarchy. To do this, select the node that you want to add the products to, and open up the **Products** section of the record. To add a single product, click the **Add** button.

This will open up a list of all the **Products** that you have configured in your system. Select the product that you want to add and click the **Select** button.

Repeat the process to add as many other products as you like to the category node, and then click the **OK** button to update the products.

If the products were not initially set up and configured as **Retail Products**, then Dynamics AX may ask you if you want to update the products with retail configurations.

If you click **Yes** then it will ask you what information you want to update on the Released Products record. In this case we will allow for negative inventory and also zero prices – although you may not want to do this in a real system.

After clicking **Update** the system will add your products to your hierarchy node. Repeat for all of your other products and then click the **Close** button on the form to finish the process.

Creating Retail Product Assortments

Products are assigned to **Stores** by creating what are called **Retail Product Assortments**. **Assortments** have two purposes. Firstly they are a grouping of products that you are going to sell, and their second role is to associate the products with **Retail Channels** that say what **Stores** they are to be sold in.

HOW TO DO IT...

Click on the **Assortments** menu item from the **Common** group of the **Retail** Area page.

This will open up the **Assortments** maintenance form. To create a new **Assortment**, click on the **Assortment** button in the **New** group of the **Assortments** ribbon bar.

If you are not already in edit mode, then click on the **Edit** button in the **Maintain** group of the **Assortments** ribbon bar. Then give your new assortment record an **Assortment ID**, and **Name.**

Then we want to assign our **Assortment** to one or more **Retail Channels**. To do that, click on the **Add line** button in the **Retail channels** section of the record.

This will open up the **Retail Organization Hierarchy** browser. You can select stores individually and add them to the Assortment by selecting them and clicking on the **Add >>** button, or you can assign stores to the **Assortment** by selecting their **Business Unit**. In this example we will save time, and just assign this assortment to all of the **Stores** that are in our parent **Business Unit**. This way, as we add more stores, then we can simply add them to the Business Unit, and then they will automatically be assigned to the **Assortment**.

Now we need to assign products to our assortment. We do this much the same way that we did with the **Retail Channels** by select the **Add line** button in the **Products** section of the record.

This will open up the **Retail Product Category** browser. We can add any node that we like and add it to the assortment.

In this example we will save time, and just assign this assortment to all of the **Stores** that are in our parent **Business Unit.** This way, as we add more stores, then we can simply add them to the Business Unit, and then they will automatically be assigned to the **Assortment.**

Now we need to assign products to our assortment. We do this much the same way that we did with the **Retail Channels** by select the **Add line** button in the **Products** section of the record.

This will open up the **Retail Product Category** browser. We can add any node that we like and add it to the assortment.

One last thing to do here on the Assortment is to set an **Effective Date**.

Once all of the products and stores have been associated with our **Assortment**, click on the **Close** button to save and publish your **Assortment**.

If you want to double check your setup, click on the **View assortment products** button from the **Inquiries** group of the **Assortments** ribbon bar.

This will show you all of the products that are part of the **Assortment**. In the **Fact Boxes** you should also see that the products are associated with a **Retail Channel** and also a **Product Assortment.**

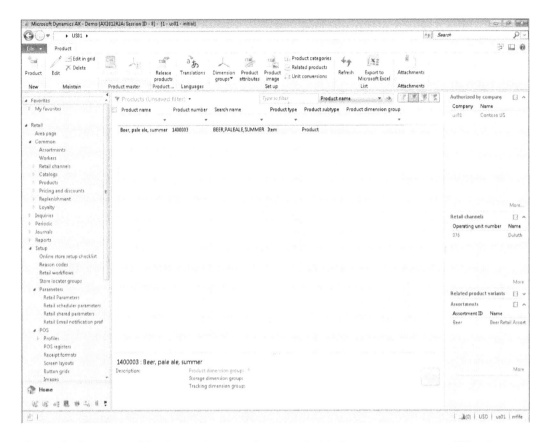

If you don't see anything here, then you have probably forgotten to set an **Effective Date** on the **Assortment.**

Processing Assortments

After creating or updating **Assortments** there is one final administrative step that you need to perform, and that is to process them. This will use the **Assortment** configurations that you have created to explode them out to the **Store** records for your POS Registers to use.

HOW TO DO IT...

Click on the **Process assortments** menu item in the **Periodic** group of the **Retail** area page.

When the update dialog pops up, click on the **OK** button to start the process.

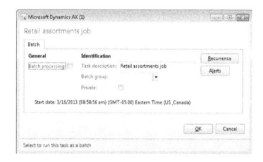

When this has finished, you will see all of the products that have been deployed out to the stores, with the item counts for the assortments.

Creating POS Terminals

Once you have all of the **Stores**, **Workers**, **Products**, and **Assortments** configured, the only thing that is stopping you from taking orders is that you don't have any **POS Registers** configured.

HOW TO DO IT...

Click on the **POS registers** menu item in the **POS/Profiles** group in the **Setup** section of the **Retail** Area page.

This will open up a list of all the **POS Registers** that you have defined in your system. To create a new register, click on the **Register** button in the **New** group of the **Register** ribbon bar.

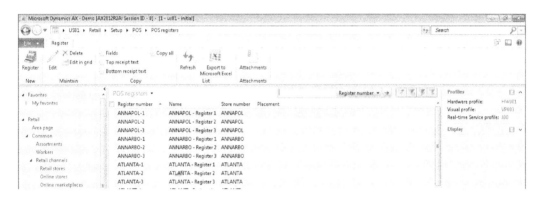

This will open up a record for your new **Register**. If you are not currently in edit mode, then click on the **Edit** button in the **Maintain** group of the **Register** ribbon bar.

Give your new register a **Register Number**, **Name**, and also a **Reference**, which will be your store. Just as with the Store and Warehouse, we are making things easier to track in these examples by using the city name as the main reference for the **Register.**

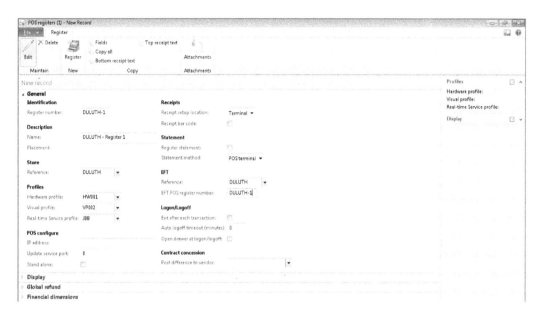

Other fields that you may want to configure include the **Hardware** and **Visual Profiles** for the **Register**.

If you want to have a custom screen layout for the register, and override the one that is defined at the **Store** level, then in the **Display** section of the record, you can assign a specific one in the **Screen layout ID** field.

Tip: If you already have some registers configured, then you can copy their configurations through the **Copy all** function in the **Copy** group of the **Registers** menu bar.

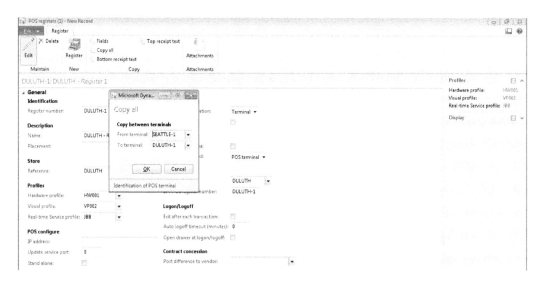

After you have finished, you can click the **Close** button to save your register configuration.

Create a POS Database

The POS Registers work are designed to work in a stand-alone manner, not requiring access to the main Dynamics AX system, so that if they loose connectivity, the workers can keep on recording sales. In order to do this, each store will have it's own database that it will run from locally. So as part of the configuration process, we need to create that database shell. That's not a big deal though because there is a utility delivered with Dynamics AX that will help you with the process.

HOW TO DO IT...

Before we can create the POS database information you first need to create the blank database within MSSQL Server.

To access the Retail Database Utility, look in the Microsoft Dynamics AX 2012 program folder for the Retail Database Utility folder.

In the dialog box that pops up, change all of the Store and Register references to point to the ones that you want to create the database for.

Before running the update, click on the Test connection button to make sure that you are able to communicate with the database.

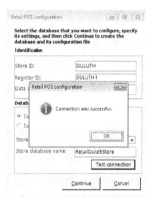

To create the Store database, just click the Continue button.

If everything worked as it should then you should be done.

If you open up SQL Management Studio, you will see your new database that the utility created for you.

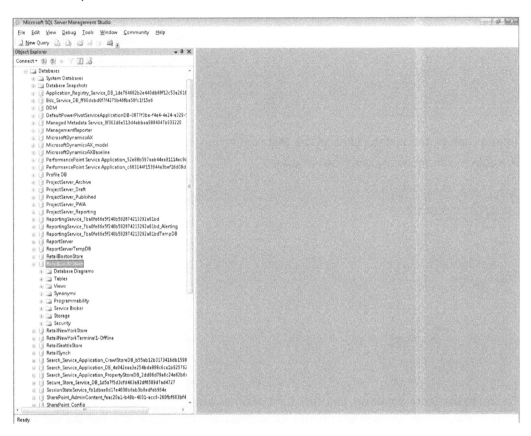

Along with all of the staging tables for the store.

Unfortunately though they are all empty, because there are a few more steps required to synchronize the data down to the store.

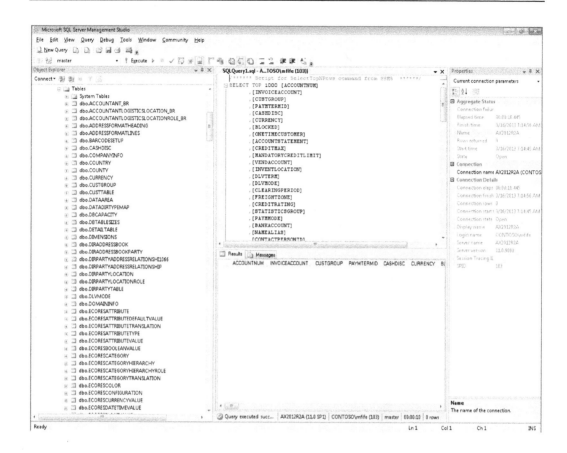

Setup POS Database Profile

Once you have a **Store database** configured you need to register it with the retail module so that it is able to use it.

HOW TO DO IT...

Click on the **Database Profiles** menu item in the **Retail scheduler/Channel Integration** group of the **Setup** section of the **Retail** Area page.

Each store database needs to be registered here with a profile. You can create a new record by clicking on the **New** button on the menu bar, although if you already have **Store Database Profiles** defined, then it's easier just to create a profile from the existing ones by clicking on the **Copy** menu item.

When you select the copy option, you just need to give your database profile a name and click the **OK** button.

Then change your **Database name** to match the new database that you have configured.

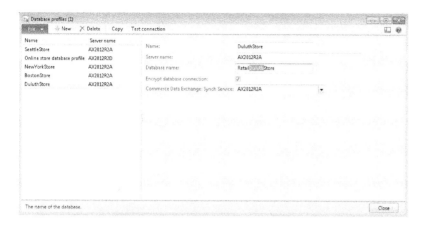

To check that the connection is correctly configured, click on **Test connection** menu item. If everything is connected correctly then the test will succeed.

Adding POS Database to Distribution Locations

In order to have Dynamics AX synchronize its data with the store locations, you need to have them configured with a **Distribution Location** which will be linked with the **Store Database**. You will use these later to define rules as to when the data is sent back and forth to them, but in this example we will show how you link the **Stores Distribution Locations** with the **Store Database**.

HOW TO DO IT...

Click on the **Distribution locations** menu item in the **Retail scheduler** folder within the **Setup** group within the **Retail** area.

Your **Store Location** should already be in the system – it is created as you create your **Store**. It will just be missing the **Database profile** and **Channel Schema**.

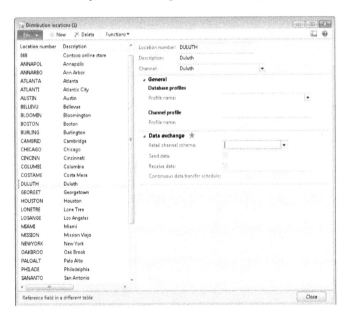

In the **Profile name** field, add the database that you registered for the store.

You should also have a value configured for the **Retail channel schema** that you can select and use.

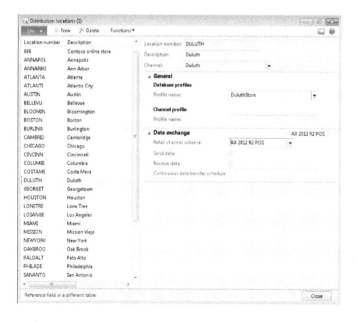

Before continuing on, select the **Test connection** option from the **Functions** menu item to make sure that everything is configured correctly.

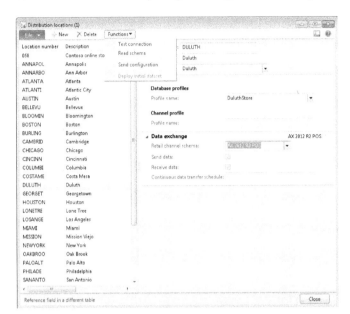

If you have everything in place, then you should get a successful message.

Finally you need to update Sync Service configuration. To do this select the **Send configuration** option from the **Functions** menu item. If all of your synchronization services are working correctly you should get a successful message notice and you are done.

Adding POS to the Distribution List

Once you have your **Store Database** created, and configured with its distribution information, there is one final configuration step that needs to be performed. The distribution location needs to be added to the default distribution list so that when the data synchronization is performed, it is included.

HOW TO DO IT...

Click on the **Distribution location list** menu item in the **Retail scheduler** folder within the **Setup** group within the **Retail** area.

Select the **Default include list** record and you will be able to see all of the **Store Distribution Locations** that will have their data synchronized.

To add your new **Store Distribution Location** to the list, click on the **Add** button in the **distribution Locations** section and select your **Store Distribution Location** that you created.

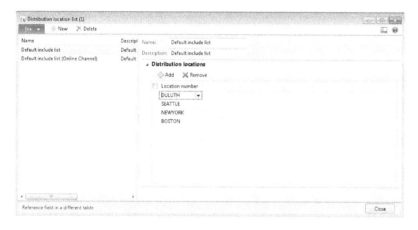

Then click **close** to save your changes.

Running Initial Data Distribution

Once all of the plumbing for the **Store** has been successfully set up, it will start synchronizing the data through the **Data Distribution Lists** that you have configured. When you have a clean store database though, you need to run an initial update to load all of the store data. The easiest way to do this is by running the **Data Distribution** schedule by hand.

HOW TO DO IT...

Click on the **Distribution schedule** menu item in the **Data distribution** folder within the **Periodic** group within the **Retail** area.

Here you will see a list of scheduled jobs that are used to distribute the data to the POS databases. Select the first job – *A-100* and then click on the **Run Directly** menu button.

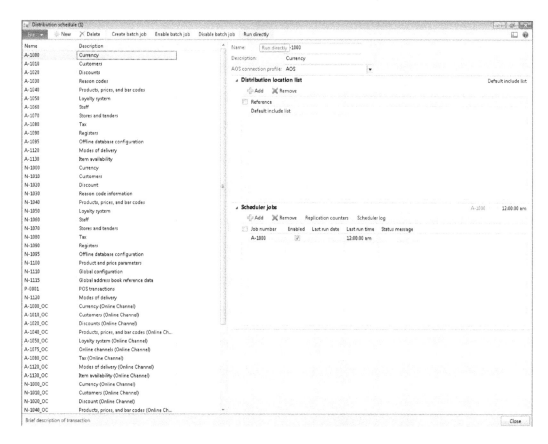

When the confirmation box shows up, select **Yes** to run the process. After you have finished the Status Message should show that the job completed successfully.

Now repeat this process for all the A jobs, and also the incremental N jobs as well, ignoring the Online Channel ones though.

Now if you look at your database in SQL Server Management Studio, you should see that your **Store Database** is populated.

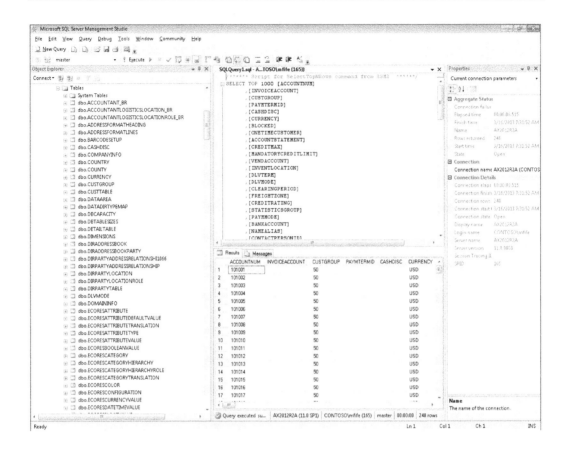

Creating A POS Shortcut

Normally you would install the Retail Point Of Sale application on it's own PC, and it would be configured to run as a single register instance. If you are running these examples from the demonstration images provided by Microsoft though you will need to hack the system a little bit so that we are able to open the right **Store Register** and attach to the correct **Store Database**.

Although you may not need to perform these steps in real life, we will show you the steps any way just in case you need to tweak the POS shotcuts.

HOW TO DO IT...

In the demonstration images, there are a number batch files, and configuration files that are run to switch registers on the fly. You should be able to find them in the "C:\Program files (x86)\Microsoft Dynamics AX\60\Retail POS" folder. We will use these to create new scripts and configuration files that point to our new **Store** and **Register**.

Start off by finding the Register Configuration files. They have the name *Pos.exe.RegisterName.config* (the .config may be hidden).

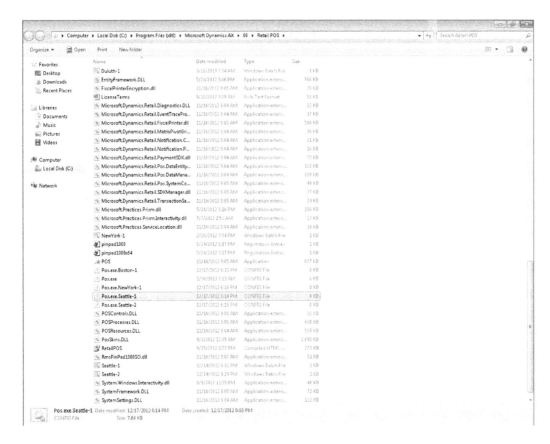

Make a copy of the file and then rename the file to match the POS Register Name that you want to open. Then Edit the file in a text editor.

There is a lot of information in the config file, but there are only a few items that you need to redirect.

First, change the database reference to be the Store database.

Then change the **StoreId**.

Change the **Register Id**.

And finally, if the Store is in a different company, then change the **DataAreaID**.

Now save and close the file.

Then find the Register batch file. They have the name *RegisterName.bat* (the .bat may be hidden). This is a batch file that changes the default configuration files to the alternate versions, allowing you to switch from one register to another.

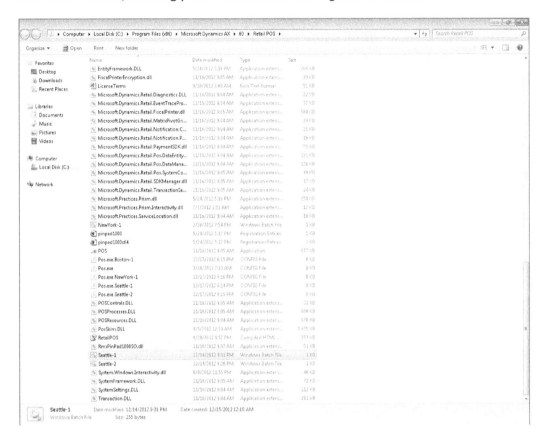

Make a copy of the file and then give it the name of the Register that you want to switch to for easy reference.

Now edit the batch file.

The batch file will be pointing to the old POS config file. Change the configuration reference to be your new Register configuration file.

Now save and close the file.

For extra credit, you can also copy any of the POS startup shortcuts that are on the demo image desktop to point to your new batch file.

HOW IT WORKS...

If you click on the shortcut, it should change the configuration file for the default POS

Register to your new configuration and send you to the login screen.

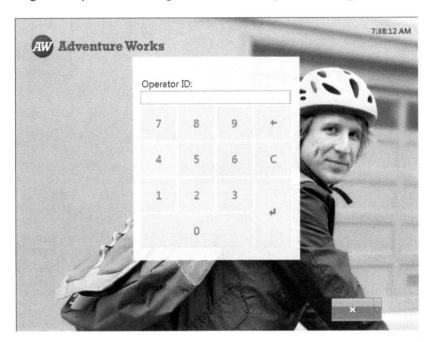

Logging Into Your POS Terminal

Once all of the configuration and setup is complete, you should be able to start using your POS Register.

HOW IT WORKS...

When you are at the Operator ID screen within POS, type in the **Worker ID** for any of the users that have been registered against the **Store** through the **Worker Address Book** that has been assigned to the **Store**.

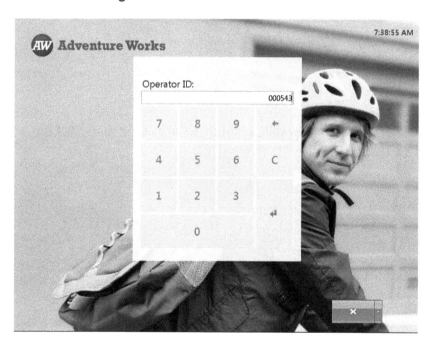

The password that you use to log into the POS Register is the password that you have defined in the Retail section of the Worker profile.

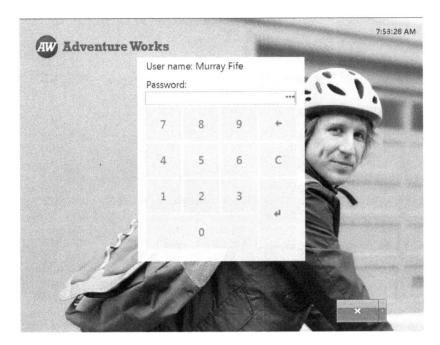

This will ask you to either Open up a new shift, or return to an existing shift. Click on **Open a new shift.**

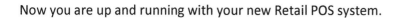

Now you are up and running with your new Retail POS system.

You can search for customers by clicking on the **Search customers** button.

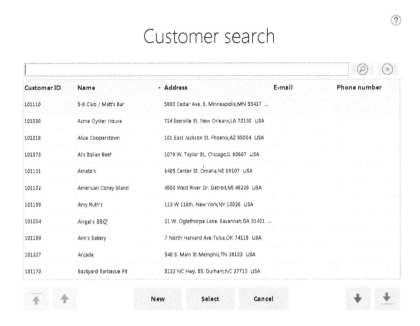

You can also perform product lookups directly from the POS system as well.

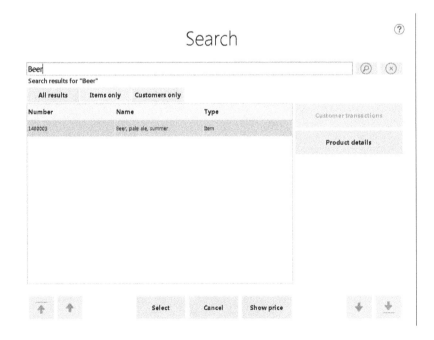

Assigning Shortcut Keys to POS Buttons

Although the POS screens are designed to be touched, you may also want to give the power POS users the ability to navigate through the screens with shortcuts and hot keys on the keyboard.

HOW TO DO IT...

There are two ways that you can update the POS buttons within Dynamics AX. The first is through the Screen layouts, and also through the Button grids. In this example we will use the first, which you can access from the **Retail** area page, by clicking on the **Screen layouts** menu item within the **POS** folder of the **Setup** group.

When the **Screen layouts** dialog box is displayed, select the layout that you want to change and click on the **Designer** button in the menu bar.

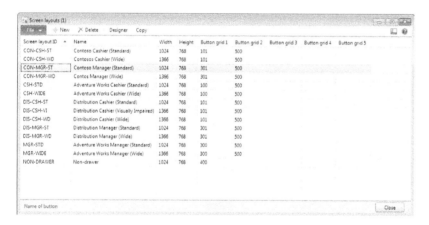

This will take you into the interactive design mode for the POS screen. Right-mouse-click on the button that you want to change and select the **Button properties** option – in this case we will change the Voids & returns.

This will open up the button properties. Now you can change the text for the button, and put an "&" in front of for the key that you want to assign the shortcut to.

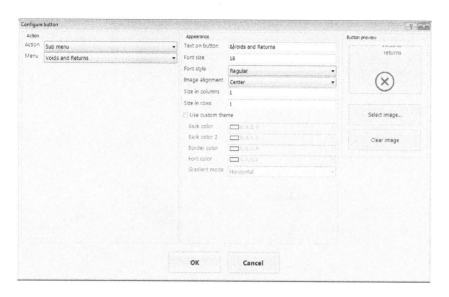

In the designer, we can continue drilling through the buttons to assign shortcuts to the submenu items as well.

In this case we will also assign the shortcut key of "V" to the *Void transaction* button.

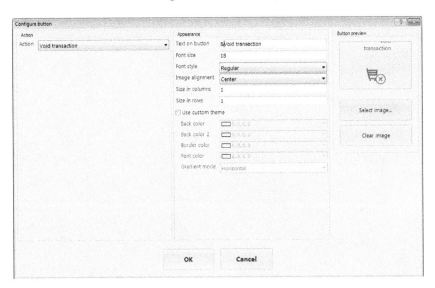

Once you have finished updating the POS screen layouts and buttons, click on the **Distribution schedule** menu item in the **Data Distribution** folder of the **Periodic** group of the **Retail** Area page.

Select the *N-1090* job and click on the **Run directly** button in the menu bar to distribute all of the design changes to all of the registers.

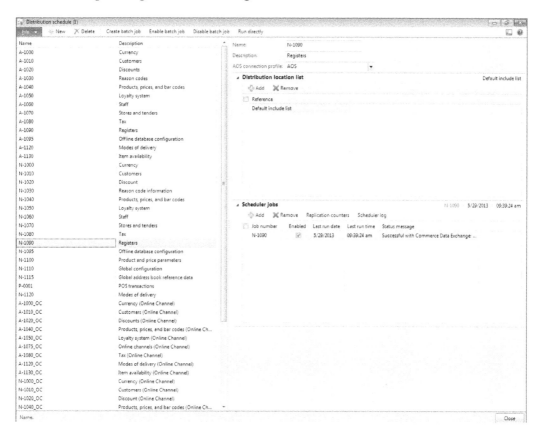

Now, when we are in the POS Register, we can quickly void a transaction by pressing ALT-V, ALT-V.

Summary

The retail module is pretty darn cool, and being able to configure and deploy a Point Of Sales system that is completely integrated with your base system, without having to purchase any more software is a great benefit. You could easily deploy registers out to PC's and tablets without much additional work.

There is still a lot more that you can do though that we did not touch on yet within this blueprint. After you have mastered the basics that we introduced here you may want to try:

- Creating custom layouts for different screen form factors
- Change the background image for the POS welcome screens
- Create variations of the POS for different users

Setting up a store has never been so easy.

Conclusion

Now that you have mastered these features, what will you do now? I hope that you will look for more that will make you even better.

Index

No index entries found.

About the Author

Murray Fife is a Microsoft Dynamics AX MVP, author of Extending Dynamics AX 2012 Cookbook, and Solution Architect at I.B.I.S. Inc with over 18 years of experience in the software industry.

Like most people in this industry he has paid his dues as a developer, an implementation consultant, a trainer, and now spend most of his days working with companies solving their problems with the Microsoft suite of products, specializing in the Dynamics® AX solutions.

EMAIL   mfife@ibisinc.com

TWITTER   @murrayfife

BLOG   http://extendingdynamicsax.com

               http://dynamicsaxtipoftheday.com

               http://atinkerersnotebook.com

SLIDESHARE http://slideshare.net/murrayfife

LINKEDIN   http://www.linkedin.com/in/murrayfife

AMAZON   http://www.amazon.com/author/murrayfife